WDLR ALBUM

'FIRST TRAIN ON VIMY RIDGE – APRIL 1917'

From a watercolour by Roy C Link

WDLR ALBUM

Compiled by Roy C Link

A unique record of British 60cm gauge
railways on the Western Front – Spring 1918

RCL Publications

WDLR ALBUM

© Authors & RCL Publications
First edition July 2014

ISBN 978-0-9565157-2-8

The editor and publisher gratefully acknowledge the permission
granted to reproduce the copyright material in this book. Every effort has
been made to trace copyright holders and to obtain their permission for
the use of copyright material. The publisher apologises for any errors
or omissions and would be grateful if notified of any corrections that should
be incorporated in future reprints or editions of this book.

Design & Typography by Roy C Link

Published by
RCL PUBLICATIONS
Cambrian Forge, Garndolbenmaen,
Gwynedd, LL51 9RX

Printed by
Lavenham Press, 47 Water Street,
Lavenham, Suffolk, CO10 9RN

CONTENTS

DEDICATED TO

Thomas Link

Lance Corporal, South Wales Borderers

One of 'the fallen'

"A FUTURE WAR...

...will be a national war which will not be settled by a decisive battle but by a long wearisome struggle with a country that will not be overcome until the whole national force is broken, and a war which will utterly exhaust our own people, even if we are victorious"

Alfred Von Schlieffen to the Kaiser – 1905

INTRODUCTION

Military Background: The Munitions Crisis of 1916: Development of the WDLR: Origins of this Album

HE 60CM GAUGE LIGHT RAILWAYS of the Great War (1914-1918) continue to exercise a fascination almost a century after their creation. Both the Allies (Great Britain, France, Russia, Italy and later the USA) and the Central Powers (Germany and the Austro-Hungarian Empire) employed narrow gauge railways for the tactical re-supply of troops in forward areas. Whilst the French and to an extent the Germans sometimes used existing light railways, the lightly built 60cm gauge lines of the British forces were unique in their concept, origins and execution.

Whereas the German Military had developed 'feldbahnen' to provide rail lines of communication in areas not served by standard gauge railways, the French had developed specialist narrow-gauge rail systems to serve the massive fortifications of their eastern frontier cities. In the closing years of the 19th century, German military railway development had been diverted to the 'feldbahn' concept by the need to develop communications in German South-West Africa. The result was the remarkable Swakopmund to Windhuk military railway, 385 km long and constructed by engineers of the German Imperial Army between 1897 and 1902 in most difficult conditions. This was, at the time, the world's longest 60cm gauge railway.

Meanwhile, in the United Kingdom three distinct threads of military railway development can be identified. The curiosity is that none of them led to, or even envisaged, the construction of large scale narrow gauge systems for battlefield replenishment in forward areas. The first and arguably most important thread was the development of railway lines of communication for the British Expeditionary Force from a port of entry to the forward bases of the force.

These lines would either be developed from the existing railway network of the host country or by new construction of standard gauge railways. The second thread was the preparation of alternative rail lines of communication in under-developed countries, particularly where climate and terrain might make standard gauge railways unfeasible. After the disastrous experience of the Red Sea campaign of 1885 (when the Royal Engineers built an 18inch gauge tramway to serve the forts and harbours of Suakin), it had been decided that 2ft 6in was the minimum acceptable gauge for the construction of any such railways in future colonial wars. As this was the favoured gauge for feeder railways in India, and because the Indian army was often responsible for such projects, the British army took little interest in narrow gauge railways from about 1905. Because of a general loss of interest in siege warfare, following the war in South Africa (1899-1902), little more was done to develop the third thread, the 18inch gauge fortification railways, after the Royal Engineers moved their railway training activities to Longmoor in 1905.

The concept of operations for the British Expeditionary

Force in 1914 envisaged the greater part of the logistic support of the Force being carried out using the French railways (which would pass into government control on the declaration of war). Initially there appeared to be no significant need for any British military railway units, the Royal Engineers contributing one railway company to the Order of Battle of the BEF. This is not the place to detail the development of trench warfare during 1914 and 1915 which led to the rapid growth of the narrow gauge trench tramways.

The Munitions Crisis of 1916

The underlying cause for the development of the trench tramways was the rapid increase in the scale and intensity of combat between the entrenched armies in Belgium and north east France. This was industrial warfare on an unimaginable scale at a moment in the progress of military technology where 'firepower' (the ability to deliver the

While the internal combustion engine developed rapidly during the Great War, its practicality, on the Western Front at least, was limited due to the often appalling conditions. Even using horses, the delivery to the front of ever larger quantities of munitions, food and other supplies became increasingly problematic – the solution was a narrow gauge railway system.

Contemporary postcard: "heavy rains have often made the British front a quagmire, and our 'Tommies' have had to put their shoulders to the wheels of ambulance and other wagons."

5. HELPING AN AMBULANCE THROUGH THE MUD
OFFICIAL PHOTOGRAPH. CROWN COPYRIGHT RESERVED

"Make-shift arrangements could not deal with such a quantity, some broad general scheme for dealing with it was needed. Neither roads nor standard gauge railway could be constructed quickly enough to follow up an advance; the solution he recommended was a very rapid development of the 60-cm. railways, which implied far larger orders for track, locomotives and wagons than had been hitherto contemplated."

Development of the WDLR

The detailed development of the system, from the first crude 'trench tramways' of 1915 has been admirably and comprehensively told elsewhere[1]. It is important to stress here a number of aspects of the development of the 'War Department Light Railways' (WDLR) – their official collective title – because the process was so different from anything which happened before or since their inception. Never previously had any group, business or government department, organised a new railway network (of any gauge) on such a grand scale and at such short notice. At a time when UK industry was already gearing up to the unprecedented demands of war production, the additional needs of the WDLR were, in some cases, beyond the capabilities of our own manufacturers. Already, in the summer of 1916, orders for locomotives were being placed with the Baldwin locomotive company in the USA. The October 1916 orders which followed, (collectively known as 'Programme B') were massive, including: 1000 miles of track, 800 steam locomotives, 2,800 bogie wagons, and a complete central repair shop. This was no ordinary

means of destruction and the degree of destruction achieved) far outweighed 'mobility' (the ability of forces to move at will around the field of combat). None of the warring nations had the means to produce and deliver munitions in the quantities now demanded by the field commanders. The rapidly developing 'Munitions Crisis' of 1915 was a political problem as much as a military one. David Lloyd-George, first as the Minister of Munitions and then as Secretary of State for War, set about solving the production aspects of the crisis in the UK.

Increased shell production would not, in itself, solve the crisis at the front. Munitions had to be delivered when and where the commanders needed them. The Prime Minister's first reaction in August 1916 was to send Eric Geddes (formerly Assistant General Manager of the North Eastern

Railway) to France to conduct:–

"...an investigation into the transport arrangements in connection with the British Expeditionary Force both at home and overseas".

It must be remembered that the BEF was now more than four times larger than it had been in 1914 and was fighting a trench-based campaign of an intensity never previously witnessed.

Geddes made many recommendations but the one which concerns us here was that forward re-supply should be by means of light railways with a network capable of delivering up to 200,000 tons of munitions per week to the troops at the front. In his *Official History of Transportation on the Western Front, 1914-1918* Colonel A M Henniker sums up the challenge thus:–

1 – 'Light Railways of the First World War'
   W J K Davies, David and Charles: Newton Abbot, 1967.

Originally part of the Railway Operating Division RE (ROD) this Hudson-Hudswell 0-6-0WT was delivered to the Western Front in May 1916, prior to the formation of the WDLR in the autumn of that year. The original numbering was in the sequence 101-18. Later, in 1917, a revision took place, under the Directorate of Light Railways (DLR) with the prefix 'LR' – these locos being re-numbered 401-418. Wagons are bogie class 'C', first produced in March 1916 as part of 'Programme A'. With no identification other than her number, No.102 is seen at Fricourt during the Somme campaign. Note one side of the cab, which only had a front sheet, is boarded over against the prevailing weather.

it is a great credit to the officers and men of the WDLR companies that they quickly melded into an efficient and hardworking force.

The last general point about the concept of the WDLR is that its birth came about during a brief 'window of opportunity', following the successful development of small internal combustion powered locomotives but before the perfection of the robust 'cross-country' pneumatic tyre. Within a decade, the all-wheel-drive, pneumatic tyred, i/c engined road truck would enter military service, at a stroke rendering the light railways obsolete whilst tracked armoured fighting vehicles (both tanks and self-propelled artillery) would restore mobility to the wider battlefield.

The Origins of this Album

So much for the concept of tactical military light railways, their origins and development. What of this album? What does it show us and why is it important?

When we examine the context in which this album was prepared, we must remember that the engineers and technical staffs of the Great War era had been brought up in the strict and formal disciplines of Victorian engineering. Similarly rigorous disciplines applied to the management of affairs of state so, whilst a global empire could be controlled by a relatively small number of officers, assisted by the almost universal electric telegraph network, achievements could only be recorded by means of written reports. The archives of the Great War are full of such reports, meticulously prepared, usually illustrated with diagrams and line drawings and supported by detailed statistical tables. Photographs however could only be incorporated in printed reports by converting them to half-tone blocks, an expensive process which could not be justified for the short printing runs required for most operational reports. It was therefore relatively common for reports to be accompanied by albums of photographic prints – not necessarily distributed to all recipients of the report's main text.

narrow gauge railway and beyond the imagination and capacity of the UK railway industry. Equally important to the success of Geddes' proposals was the creation and training of the military units to run the WDLR. The Royal Engineers, to whom this responsibility fell, were already engaged in a long-running campaign to extract sufficient trained railwaymen from the UK main line railways to man the burgeoning RE (Transportation) Service.

Despite a number of imaginative short-cuts by the management (including widespread employment of women and the training of existing railway clerks as signalmen,

guards and shunters), this skill shortage remained. A significant number of volunteers from the colonies and from British companies in South America helped to fill the gaps whilst others with backgrounds in traction-engine driving or tramway employment were engaged to run the new light railways. Key senior NCO appointments were often filled by promoting suitable sappers already employed in the Railway Operating Division (ROD). Finally, it should not be forgotten that many of the men employed on the WDLR had been downgraded from front-line duties due to injury or sickness. Bearing in mind this diversity of backgrounds,

This album is a survivor of one such report, a survivor orphaned by many years of well-intentioned salvage drives, clear-outs and the like. Even if the main report was selected for inclusion in a War Office 'Registered File', its survival depended on the record-keeping enthusiasm of its parent Branch or Directorate. The War Office was never really successful at archive building. By its nature, its busiest periods were in times of conflict when the tiny peace organisation was boosted by an influx of temporary staff and the key personnel, naturally, pre-occupied with the fighting. So there exists a formal and official system for units to deposit mandatory 'War Diaries' on a regular basis.

The album measures 21 x 11 inches, has 61 individual leaves, all post bound. Each leaf, apart from the first, which bears the title 'FRANCE – Light Railway Construction', carries two or more whole plate prints. These were taken directly off the original negatives and have been individually scanned and edited using modern digital technology to bring out as much detail as possible. There is only minimum captioning, some of the images having no caption at all – and are marked 'Untitled' in the pages that follow. Where dated, it is always '7th March 1918'.

These are then supposed to be held as an official record. Other papers, reports and the like depend for their survival on the goodwill (and sense of history) of clerks and staff at all levels within the bureaucracy.

In this respect the WDLR was not well served. Effectively it became a separate organisation within the overall structure of military railways at war and was almost entirely staffed by temporary (later conscripted) officers and men. During 50 years of research into military railways in the British army I have only come across one peace-time RE (Transportation) officer who had any experience with the Light Railway Operating Companies during World War One. At the end of the conflict, the men were quickly demobilised to return to their previous civilian employment and the surplus equipment was sold off (always at a loss and usually for scrap). Other than the few surviving war diaries now in the National Archive, very little remains to record the achievements of the WDLR.

The album itself survived simply as a curiosity. It was not considered relevant to the various museum displays created at Longmoor after World War 2 so it lay, forgotten, in a store cupboard in Technical Policy Wing (TPW) – the branch of HQ Transportation Centre RE at Longmoor responsible for managing the railway and ports equipment inventory of the Royal Engineers. Following the creation of the Royal Corps of Transport in 1965 TPW became part of the new Army School of Transport until it too was abolished in 1973. At this point TPW simply ceased to exist, its various functions being divided up between other staff branches. Its historical records were no one's responsibility and no museum wanted their accumulated papers.

Tipped off as to what was likely to happen, Major 'Nic' Carter and myself found ourselves one day outside the TPW offices standing beside the skip into which the clerks were dumping the contents of their offices. That which somehow failed to land in the skip was taken home and sorted as best we could. At the time our top priority was the story of Longmoor itself as we were engaged in writing our history of the then recently closed Longmoor Military Railway.[2] Very little selection was possible and it was only my personal interest in narrow gauge railways, stemming from the revival of the Festiniog Railway, which saved this item. A later attempt to find it a home in the Royal Corps of Transport Museum was rebuffed with the remark –

"...we've got plenty of stuff on trains!"

Over the ensuing forty years the album was carried from posting to posting until, at last, its "Cinderella Moment" came. Roy Link shares my interest in the WDLR and has the 21st century skills to bring this unique album to life for the wider public it deserves. I hope it will give pleasure and interest to the ever-growing band of enthusiastic amateurs who have so diligently researched the history of the WDLR and their associated equipment, translating the information into beautiful models in many scales. Because the album has for so long been separated from its parent report, it has not been possible to pinpoint the majority of locations. Nevertheless, I hope it will be of interest as a collective impression of the War Department Light Railways at their zenith in the early spring of 1918.

Colonel David W Ronald
Helensburgh, May 2012

2 – 'The Longmoor Military Railway';
D W Ronald & R J Carter; David and Charles, Newton Abbot; 1974

CHAPTER ONE
MAKING TRACKS

Development: Track: Types used: Tracklaying: Construction & Maintenance

NTIL THE MIDDLE OF 1916 the 60cm (Decauville) lines were not developed to any great extent. Those in operation were constructed of very light rails (9LB per yard) and laid as tramways, upon which vehicles were propelled by man-power. Later in the year, however, a heavier type of rail was requisitioned for use on lines in advance of railheads, but it was not until towards the end of the year that any general development took place.

The Commander-in-Chief then decided to adopt a complete system of light railways for the distribution and conveyance of ammunition and other stores beyond railhead to the gun positions and towards the trenches, and also for the conveyance of roadstone. Accordingly, 1,000 miles of 20LB track was ordered, together with a large number of steam and petrol locomotives and wagons. This decision also led to the adoption of schemes for the provision of workshops and equipment for the erection and maintenance of light railway stock, whilst the question of water supply was taken in hand. The whole of the organisation was placed under the control of Brigadier-General Twining, RE, who was appointed Director of Light Railways and Roads.

TRACK
The light railway system developed rapidly. Whilst only 96 miles of railway were being operated at the end of 1916, the mileage increased to 815 by the end of 1917 and, whilst this was subsequently extended in the early months of 1918, the fluctuations in the campaign led to some being lost and then regained, the net result being that, in October, 1918, 800 route-miles were being worked.

During the year 1917, 1,022 miles of track were laid, whilst during 1918, 768 miles were laid, and 580 miles reconstructed. As the armies advanced, both in 1917 and 1918, sections of the line were dismantled if not required for salvage purposes, the track being replaced in stock or sent on ahead for new constructions. In December, 1916, there were no 20LB rails in stock, whereas at the end of 1917, despite the large amount of construction, there was a reserve of 200 miles at the depots.

In following up the advance, many remarkable performances were achieved. In the Fourth Army area, for example, a demolished timber viaduct, 250ft long, was reconstructed and available for traffic in 48 hours. On August 8, 1918, the attack in the Fourth Army area resulted in the recently-constructed system being left behind and becoming practically valueless for army purposes. Advantage was, however, taken of track and rolling-stock recovered from the enemy to open up a new system to follow up the advancing troops. Tractors were sent by road, and some 15 miles of line were being operated on August 11, six miles in advance of what had been the front-line trenches two days previously. In consequence of this rapid extension of lines, supplies were able closely to follow up the advancing troops. For instance, ammunition, supplies, etc., were conveyed to Passchendaele, and wounded brought back within 60 hours of the occupation. Again, ammunition was being delivered at Achiet-le Grand four days after the first attack.

The Railway Gazette, September 21st, 1920

TYPES OF TRACK EMPLOYED

9LB TRACK

This was the original War Office track, the design of which had not been altered since first it was brought into use with the British Expeditionary Force. This type of track was used for laying short isolated lines and battery feeders, and in very few cases were 9LB per yard lines or spurs connected to the light railway system with a physical connection. Considerable quantities of this type of track were supplied to miscellaneous works, such as quarries, concrete factories, saw mills, dumps, etc.

The main drawback in its design was the method of jointing two adjacent rails, which caused delays in laying unless it was very carefully assembled and laid with the correct number of curve lengths.

9LB THEAKSTON CLAW JOINT TRACK

This was not actually put into general use, but supplies arrived in the country within a few weeks of the termination of Foreways existence as a construction organization. It was designed with the dual purpose of getting over the difficulty mentioned in the preceding paragraph and to save steel, due to the scarcity of this material.

Ten miles of this track was sent to France, but no actual tests were made other than at the Training School. These proved satisfactory, with the exception that, with rough handling, the distance rods broke at the shoulder.

16LB TRACK

This was originally intended as a replacement for the early 9LB per yard rail but orders were soon amended to 20LB rail. Such 16LB rail as there was, became popular on trench tramways.

Above: Hudson 9LB per yard pre-fabricated track panel.

Below: Full size rail sections – shown with fishplates and bolt.

20LB TRACK

This track equipment was the standard War Office type composed of British Standard (BS) flat bottom rails weighing 20LB per yard, these being joined by a bar fish-plate, with four fish-bolts, and supported by pressed steel sleepers, to which the rails are clipped. There were two types – A and B. Type A consisted of 1,682 steel sleepers and 1,288 wood ties per mile of track, and was only used in

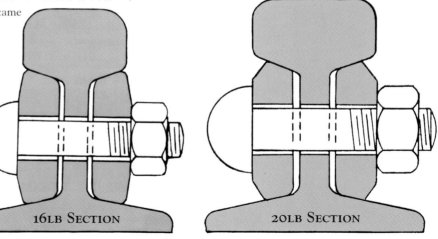

9LB SECTION   16LB SECTION   20LB SECTION

Chinese Labour Battalion Assembling Track

A six man crew repairing panels of 20lb track sections on steel sleepers for further use. They are shown checking the gauge and tightening the rail clips. In the foreground is one of the three piece 20lb turnouts supplied under supply Programme B. As the war progressed, there was an ever increasing requirement for non-combatant manpower, resulting in the formation of 'Labour Battalions'. Newspaper adverts were placed to generate recruits – see right.

Chinese labour arrived in France early in 1917 and numbers eventually reached nearly 100,000 men. Despite being under the control of British officers and NCOs, the language barrier meant that Chinese 'foremen' gave the men their instructions and supervised the work. When Companies were formed to cover particular skills, foreign labourers were allowed to take skill tests. Eventually 2,000 Chinese were taken into the Corps of Royal Engineers specifically dealing with railway maintenance and construction.

Collection: Bob Barlow

Above: 20LB rail – Hudson pressed steel
sleeper with closed ends. Extra wide section
suitable for use on soft ground.

special cases where the standard steel sleeper did not give
sufficient bearing and grip on the road bed, as in swampy,
water-logged country. Type B consisted of all-steel sleepers
(2,970 per mile), and about 90% of the track laid was with
this type. It was not until the middle of 1918 that turn-
tables for this track were available, and a few of these were
put in use in special lay-outs as in large workshops; this
turn-table was 5 ft in diam., and designed for a load of 3½
tons, and would turn 20HP tractors and all rolling stock
except bogies.

MONORAIL TRACK

A considerable number of monorail trucks (see page 218)
were available, and many were issued to Armies, these
being invariably run on 60cm track; some attempts were
made to construct monorail track by means of spiking 9LB
rails down to short wooden sleepers. This arrangement did
not give very satisfactory results, especially at the joints,
and it was therefore decided to use special steel monorail
sleepers in conjunction with the Theakston Claw Joint
described in a preceding paragraph. Some 10,000
(six miles) were ordered on September 4th,
1918 but, before any could be delivered, it was
decided to cancel the indent, owing to the
Armistice.   – RE Papers

Above: Apart from the pre-fabricated track on steel sleepers a
large quantity of 20LB per yard rail for fixing to timber sleepers
was supplied. The rail itself was sent out to the front in five
metre lengths, to be cut and curved 'in the field'. Plain dog
spikes were used to fix the rail down, without baseplates
except on turnouts. With regard to the latter, sets
of parts for the heel end, comprising stock and
tongue rails, ready planed, with fixings were
accompanied by a crossing (see right). This
latter came fully assembled on a steel plate,
ready to fix in place.

Below: 20lb rail –Hudson 'Special Turnout' built in three
sections on steel sleepers with closed ends. Hudson's
claimed "8,000 such turnouts supplied by us
for use in the Great War". One such
can be seen on page 3.

Why 60cm Gauge?

The first Light Railway (as distinct from trench tramways)
worked by the British was a 60cm gauge line laid by the
French in an area subsequently taken over by the British. The
choice of 60cm gauge for lines constructed later was based mainly
on the fact that the French had adopted that gauge and that a certain
amount of second-hand track and rolling stock was obtainable in France.
When, towards the end of 1916, it was decided to introduce light railways
along the whole British Front there was already a considerable mileage of
60cm lines in use; it was considered that metre gauge would be unduly heavy,
take too long to construct, and would not
be flexible enough to reach the delivery
point. Certain authorities at home
considered that the gauge chosen should
have been 2ft 6ins – a gauge chosen by the
War Office several years before the war as
the gauge for siege railways, of which there
was a small reserve of track and rolling
stock. There were, however, obvious
disadvantages in introducing a fourth
gauge among the existing standard, metre
and 60cm lines.
– Transportation on the Western Front
Col. A M Henniker

Light Railway construction through shell torn area East of Ypres – 7th March 1918

Laying-Out. Centre line to be marked out on a route previously chosen. Three men will be required for this purpose, who will use a rope or length of telephone wire of known length up to 330 ft (marked plainly in the middle), to be used for marking straights. Also, note the men filling sandbags (right foreground) these were used as packing around steel 'Armco' culvert sections – one runs diagonally through the track foundation shown, from the centre of the photograph to the foreground. The upper rim of the metal section is just visible to the left of the vertical shovel.

LIGHT RAILWAYS, SECOND ARMY
Detailed Instructions
Covering Surveys, Construction and Maintenance

 LMOST INEVITABLY, the Army, faced with large numbers of British, plus Canadian and Australian railwaymen (and non-railwaymen), would seek to impose military procedure and discipline. There was sense in this as, while many coming from a railway background had extensive knowledge and experience, they were mixed in with others with little or no experience. Plus they would have been deeply partisan as regards how things were done on 'their line' – which would cause confusion and possible dissent if not controlled. To this end, the booklet here was produced and, given the circumstances, the text, reproduced below, makes interesting reading. It shows a degree of understanding and sensitivity regarding experienced railwaymen and their views tempered with the needs of warfare.

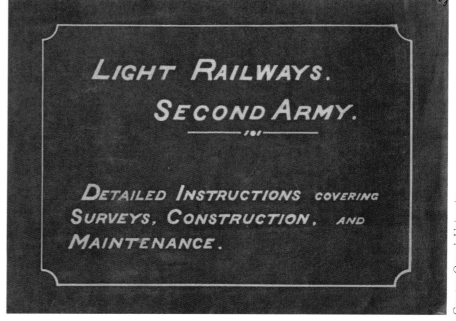

Courtesy Queen's University

The booklet comprised a text section, plus an appendix of diagrams (reproduced on later pages) and tables. The original was produced from sheets of linen blueprint, hence the cloth texture visible in some of the images. For clarity, the text pages have been reset, the content being as follows:

"Instructions contained herein, have in their object, saving time by avoiding delays, standardising the work and beating the Bosche. There is no intention to restrict good railway

NOTE: The Second Army was formed on 26 December 1914, as part of the British Army, when the British Expeditionary Force required dividing due to becoming too big to administrate. Second Army spent most of the war positioned around the Ypres salient. In 1919 it was reconstituted as the British Army of the Rhine.

practice by railway units and suggested improvements will always receive careful consideration of ADLR and his staff.

Lt Col H L Bodwell ADLR
Major W G Swan LRCE
Capt K H Smith ALRCE

SURVEYS

1 – Route Maps. For all mainline surveys, a route map showing the approximate location, will be provided by the ADLR. The location will follow the line laid down as nearly as is possible.

2 – Location. In general, the location of main lines will be preceded by a reconnaissance of the route, and running of a preliminary survey or trial line. If any particular

difficulty presents itself in the reconnaissance, same should be referred at once to ADLR or his engineer. Profiles of preliminary line should be sent to the ADLR as frequently as possible, showing daily progress.

3 – Grades and Curvature. Unless otherwise ordered ruling gradient for main line shall be 1% compensated, and curvature shall not exceed 15° per 100 feet, in sharpness. There will be no velocity grades as speed does not warrant same. Compensation for curvature will be ·02 per degree.

4 – Plans, Profiles Etc. Plans shall be plotted on scale 200ft to 1inch and should contain all available information showing nature of ground, property lines (where these

Continued on page 10…

Untitled

*As page five. To provide culverts through the formation,
'Armco' corrugated iron tube was used – as seen here.*

Construction troops grading – 7th March 1918

Forming. All available men should be placed on this work, and should be split into gangs as follows: 10% marking out and lining out inner edges of ditches, 6ft at least from centre peg on each side. Men should then be put to work on the line marked out at a distance of 10ft apart on each side of track, one side having one extra man in order to stagger the positions. The spoil from the ditches is thrown into the centre of track. Six men, evenly spaced, work on the formation, levelling off and forming to required width. All the men are wearing 'Brodie' steel helmets and are carrying their gas-mask bags, so this work was being undertaken in a forward area.

Construction troops laying steel – 7th March 1918

Rail-Laying. The first truck-load of material should be at railhead with eight men to handle the track panel; two men to fish joints; two men pushing truck and helping generally until truck is unloaded. The men handling the panel move out first, then the fasteners; the next panel is taken off the wagon and passed over the newly laid track and the process repeated. Two men commence, immediately after second panel is laid, completing fastening. The sergeant on the left and the two men kneeling (centre front) are not RE and most likely part of a construction working party from an infantry battalion. This was one of the standard chores imposed on the infantry during their time out of the front line – they were also detailed for loading stores, construction of camps etc.

Continued from page 6…

exist), buildings, roads, broad gauge lines, streams etc, as shown in appendix page 1. Profiles will be plotted on scales of 200ft–1in horizontal and 10ft–1in vertically, as per type shown in appendix, page 2. Artillery trace shall aways accompany plan and profile showing exact map location of proposed lines.

5 – General. Quantity of sleepers should not exceed 3000 per mile. Long cuttings should be avoided, especially in the forward area. Lines should not be located in front of artillery positions, if suitable line can be found in the rear. Level crossings of broad gauge lines should be 90°, 75°, 60° or 45°. Main lines should not parallel roads at a lesser distance than 200yds. Location of main lines should not be influenced by the desire to serve individual batteries. Yard and station plans shall be plotted on a scale of 40ft – 1in, unless otherwise ordered.

CONSTRUCTION

1 – Grading. The three main principles of railroading in Flanders are: drainage, drainage and more drainage.

No construction of any kind will be undertaken, until authority to commence same has been received from ADLR or his engineer. Dimensions for cuttings and embankments shall follow standard sections shown in appendix page 6. Earth slopes shall be 1½:1, unless otherwise ordered.

Dimensions of embankments and cuttings, <u>must not</u> be less than standard dimensions for finished work. Where metre gauge sleepers are used, the width of formation will be increased one foot on both cuttings and embankments. A good and sufficient berm shall be left between borrow pits and toe of slope of embankments.

Greatest care will be taken to see that culverts are properly bedded and are sufficiently low to take care of drainage. If possible, they should be laid at a right angle

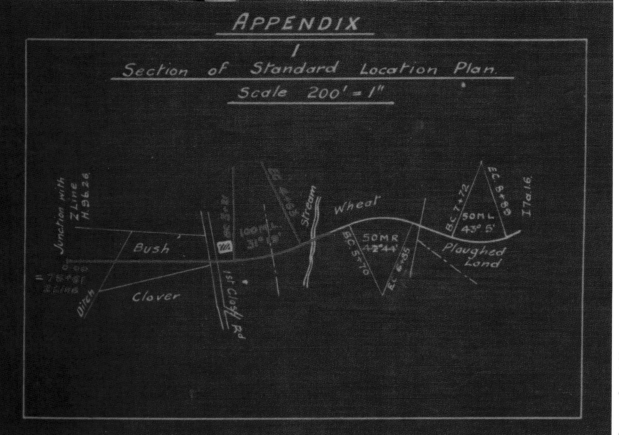

to the centre line and reasonable diversions to drainage courses may be made, in order to accomplish this. Concrete pipe, corrugated iron pipe, or timber, will be supplied, depending on the dimensions required and the stock available. Wooden culverts will be built according to standard, as shown in appendix page 7.

2 – Bridges. Bridges will be avoided wherever possible in the

forward areas, because of vulnerability. In general, where a single span only is required, steel 'I' beams will be supplied up to a span of 18 feet. Beyond this length of clear span and where two or more spans are required, wood stringers 9 x 18ins or 18 x 16ins will be used. Frame bents or wooden cribs will be used for foundations but, wherever these are unsuitable for permanent foundations, pile foundations will be driven as soon as possible by track driver and a

Construction troops laying steel – 7th March 1918

In cases where an obstruction such as a large shell crater is met, the following method of continuing track-laying should be adopted. A short curve is laid (not fastened) to turn out from the straight (and if necessary a straight length following this), then a reverse curve is laid to lead back on a parallel line. The truck-load of track is then pushed on and the curves pegged up, reversed and placed on the other end of the straight to meet the continuation of the original line. The truck is then pushed on and track-laying goes on as before. Meanwhile the obstruction is filled in or removed.

Length of span in feet	number of							
	6ins I beams	8ins I beams	10ins I beams	75lb Rails	9 x 18ins wooden stringers	8 x 16ins wooden stringers	10 x 14ins wooden stringers	12 x 12ins wooden stringers
10	4	2	2	6	2	2	2	2
12	6	2	2	8	2	2	2	2
15	8	3	2	10	2	2	3	3
18	–	4	2	–	2	3	3	3
21	–	–	3	–	2	3	3	3
25	–	–	–	–	3	4	4	4
30	–	–	–	–	3	4	–	–

permanent record of driving kept in record book supplied by ADLR. All bridges will be built to conform as nearly as possible to the standard shown in appendix page 8. Steel rails may be used in an emergency on new lines, but no steel of less than 75LBS per yard should be considered. The table above should be used in ordering material for variable bridge spans:

TRACKLAYING & BALLASTING

1 – Tracklaying. Track shall be laid with staggered or broken joints with nine sleepers per five metre rail length. The joints will be supported, not suspended. (This does not apply to assembled track, which must be laid with even joints and 2929 steel sleepers per mile). Where 45LB steel is used with metre gauge sleepers, spacing for sleepers shall be 2ft 6ins centre to centre. Care shall be taken to lay sleepers

Degree of Curvature	Increased Gauge	Superelevation
35° (50m Rad)	¾in	1in
17° 50' (100m Rad)	½in	¾in
10° and under	½in	½in

square to the track. Sleepers shall be spiked as shown in appendix page 9. No modifications will answer. Sleeper plates shall be used, two per sleeper (and rails curved in standard rail bender), on all curves of a lesser radius than 100 metres. Gauging will be accurate. The table below left shall be used for gauge and super-elevation on curves.

2 – Ballasting. Ballasting shall be done with sand, mine earth, or broken brick, as available. Mixture of sand and mine earth preferred. The average lift shall be 6ins under sleeper, to be made in to lifts of 3ins each, well tamped. Standard section as shown in appendix page 9 shall be followed. Track shall be lined after final lift, before any trimming is done.

Particular attention shall be given to provide even bearing where steel sleepers are used. Earth shall on no account be packed on the ballast shoulder, it stops drainage of ballast.

MAINTENANCE

Wherever possible, maintenance shall be carried on by permanent section gangs, allotted to given sections of lines. In normal times an average of 12 men per mile, should

cover this work from front to rear. In the forward area, a small amount of repair material should be kept at given recognised sidings, not more than one mile apart. A very small number of wood sleepers should be kept forward, as these are likely to take fire.

Main points of maintenance are surfacing, (picking up low spots, and not a constant general re-lifting). Maintenance of track to gauge and line, tightening bolts, joints full bolted and respiking where necessary. Particular attention to keep turnouts in proper running order.

GENERAL

Rolling stock and power will be supplied to construction units, according to necessity and stock available. Demands covering the above will be made to LRCE who will arrange. Wherever possible, the power so supplied should be manned by the construction units themselves. Where operating personnel are supplied, these will be attached to the construction unit for duty, discipline and rations.

Responsibility for care of power and rolling stock will rest with the construction units, but same will be inspected by the locomotive superintendant or his representative, whenever requested. Oil, coal, petrol, etc, will be supplied by Loco Supt, at points to be arranged directly with him. SLR will supply instructions on care of rolling stock on demand.

Wagons must not be loaded with ballast or other material, until doors have been properly fastened. Responsibility for this must be allotted and disciplinary action taken for failure to comply. Wagon axles should be greased at least once a week.

Track may be cut for repairs, only by permission of the District Controller, who will first obtain permission of CTC.

Operating rules will apply throughout to construction trains. Construction cars shall not be left overnight in passing sidings, nor group station spurs, nor at any forward

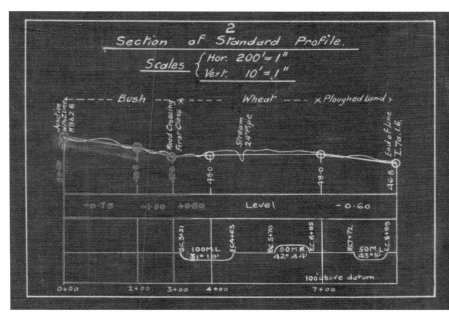

2

Section of Standard Profile.

Scales { Hor. 200'=1" / Vert. 10'=1" }

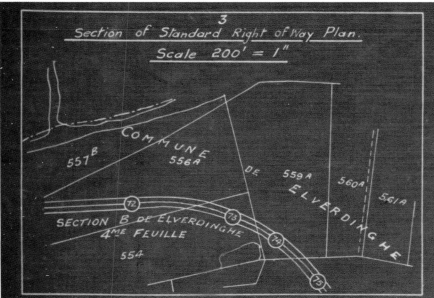

3

Section of Standard Right of Way Plan.

Scale 200' = 1"

4

Table to accompany Standard Right-of-Way Plan

NAME OF COMMUNE	ITEM NUMBER	CHAINAGE ON CENTRE LINE (METRES)		No. ON PLAN CADASTRAL	SIGN OF SECTION ON PLAN CADASTRAL	DATE OF ENTRY
	72	4415	4581	556^A		Oct 21/1915
	73	4581	4638	554		"
	74	4638	4686	559^A	SECTION	"
COMMUNE	75	4686	4939	543^A	B	"
	76	4939	5006	542		"
	77	5006	5068	541	4me FEUILLE	"
	78	5068	5263	537		"
	79	5263	5393	537BIS		"
DE	ELVERDINGHE EXTENSION					
	1	58	74	536	SECTION	June 3rd/1915
	2	74	220	517	B	"
	3	220	265	516		"
ELVERDINGHE	4	265	310		4me FEUILLE	"
	5	310				"

5

Continuation of Table to accompany Standard R.-of-W. Plan.

NATURE OF CROPS	STATE OF CROPS	LIMIT OF ENCROACHMENT LEFT SIDE	RIGHT SIDE	AREA OF ENCROACHMENT	LIMITS OF ACQUISITION LEFT SIDE	RIGHT SIDE	AREA OF ACQUISITION ARES	CENTS	REMARKS
UNCULTIVATED					7.0 4.25	7.0 4.25	16	12	
RYE GRASS					4.25 6.0	4.25 6.0	5	85	
UNCULTIVATED					4.25 4.25	4.25 4.25	4	08	
PASTURE					4.25 4.25	4.25 4.25	22	77	
UNCULTIVATED					4.25 6.0	5.0 6.0	7	21	
"					6.0 6.0	6.0 6.0	7	44	
"					6.0 4.25	6.0 6.0	22	34	
					4.25 6.0	6.0 7.0	14	34	
CHICORY					4.25 4.25	BRY BRY	1	30	
"					7.0 4.25	4.25 4.25	11	43	
OATS					4.25 6.0	4.25 6.0	4	53	

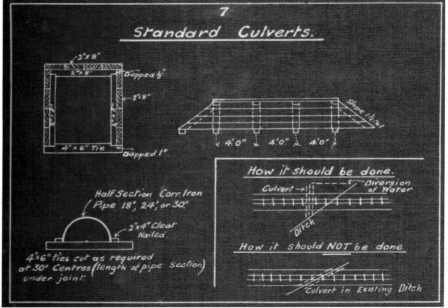

Courtesy Queen's University

point where same shall be liable to destruction by enemy shell fire.

Requests for power and rolling stock should be kept to a minimum. Wheels are round, to turn, and any rolling stock found unnecessary should be turned over at once to the Operating Department. Arrangements to increase or decrease stock must be made through LRCE.

Light railway sectional stores will provide all available materials for construction and maintenance. All indents for tools and materials will be made through LRCE Stores Officer, who will supply on his approval only. No materials for camp construction will be supplied. Railway Units will draw materials from Corps.

Only 20HP and 40HP tractors and Hudson or Barclay locomotives should be worked over new track. Petrol Electrics and other types of locomotive, should not be worked over un-ballasted track. Going over the top with PEs is not permitted until the ground is thoroughly reconnoitred, since some good work has been done with this type of war engine, in spite of remarks to the contrary."

APPENDIX DRAWINGS

Pages 1 to 22 were single sheet drawings, providing illustrations for the foregoing text. The blueprint process did not always give a sharp reproduction, particularly if the master was not firmly in contact with the base medium. The following appendix pages have been omitted:

16 – Colours to be used on Progress Profiles to denote progress of work.

The drawings and diagrams show the ideal to the aimed for, rather than necessarily achieved. Wherever possible, when time allowed, the instructions would be followed as closely as possible, with military discipline re-inforcing crucial detail. The men involved in the work of laying down, operating and maintaining the light railways were as pushed and stressed as much as those in the front line, on occasion.

Note that, in the forgoing and elsewhere, 'broad gauge' means standard 4ft 8½ins (standard gauge).

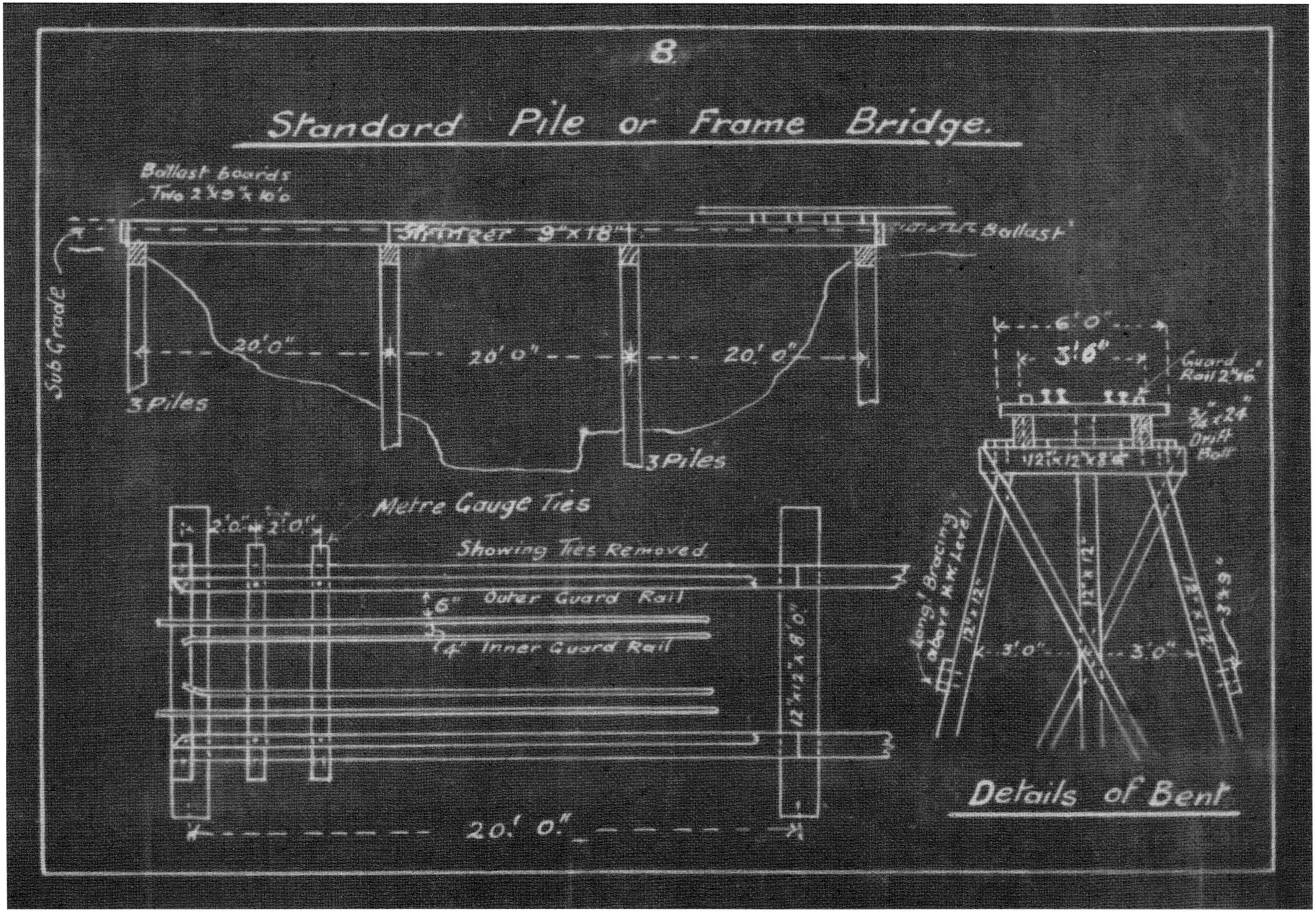
8
Standard Pile or Frame Bridge.
Ballast boards Two 2"x9"x10'0
Stringer 9"x18"
Ballast
Sub Grade
20'0"
20'0"
20'0"
3 Piles
3 Piles
6'0"
3'6"
Guard Rail 2"x6"
3/4"x24" Drift Bolt
12"x12"x8'6"
Metre Gauge Ties
2'0"
2'0"
Showing Ties Removed
6" Outer Guard Rail
4" Inner Guard Rail
12"x12"x8'0"
Long'l Bracing above H.W. Level
12"x12"
12"x12"
12"x12"
3'0"
3'0"
20'0"
Details of Bent

Courtesy Queen's University

9.

Standard Tracklaying and Ballasting.

2'0" 2'0" 2'0" 2'0"

Court Martial offence to put
earth on toe of Ballast Slope

10'0"
6'6"

Ballast

With L.R. Ties   6"lift

Ballast

With Metre Gauge Ties

Double Track   10' 0"

Ballast   Ballast

6"lift

Sub-grade to act as drainage Channel.
DO NOT deepen, or fill, except in case of Yards.

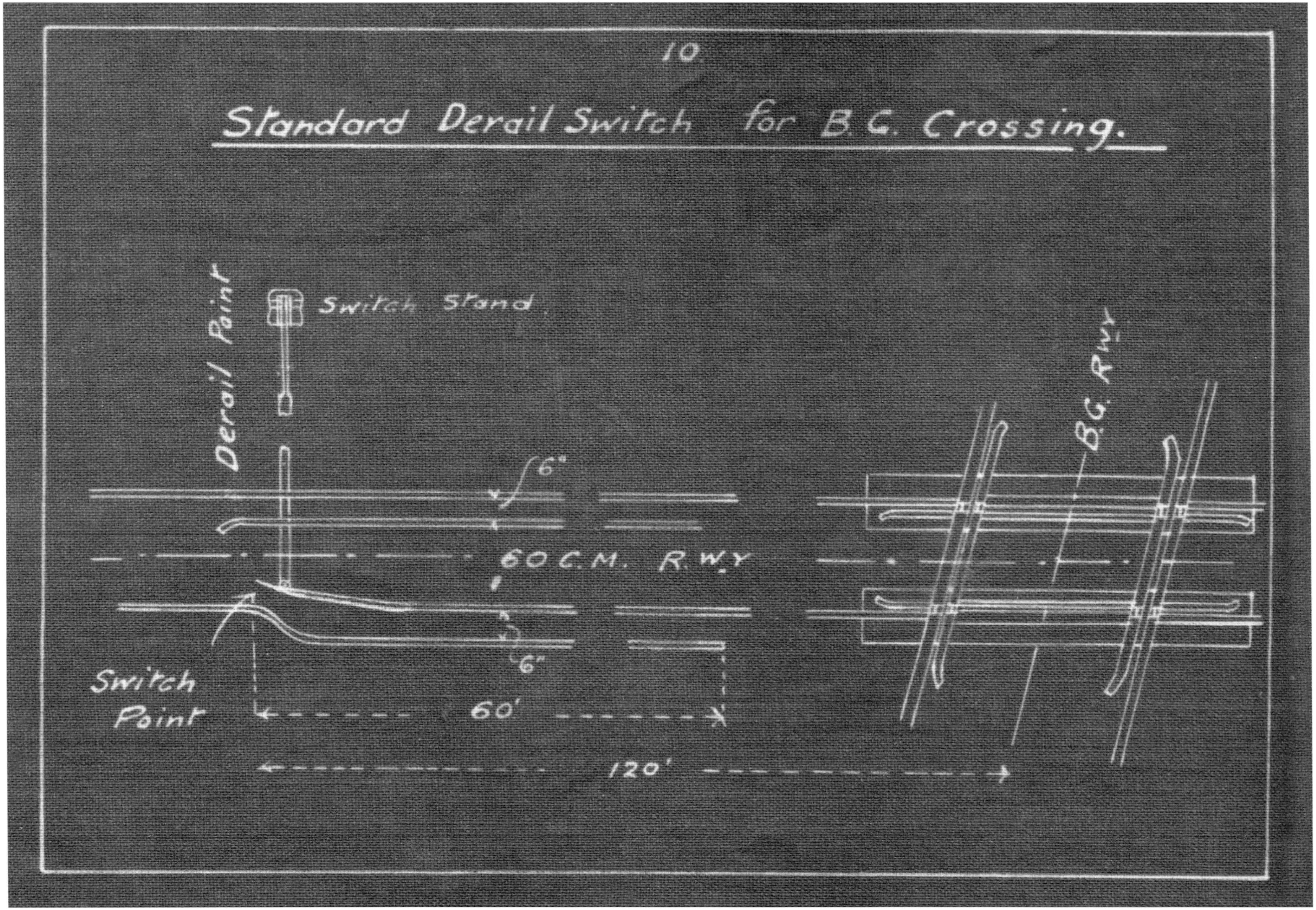

Courtesy Queen's University

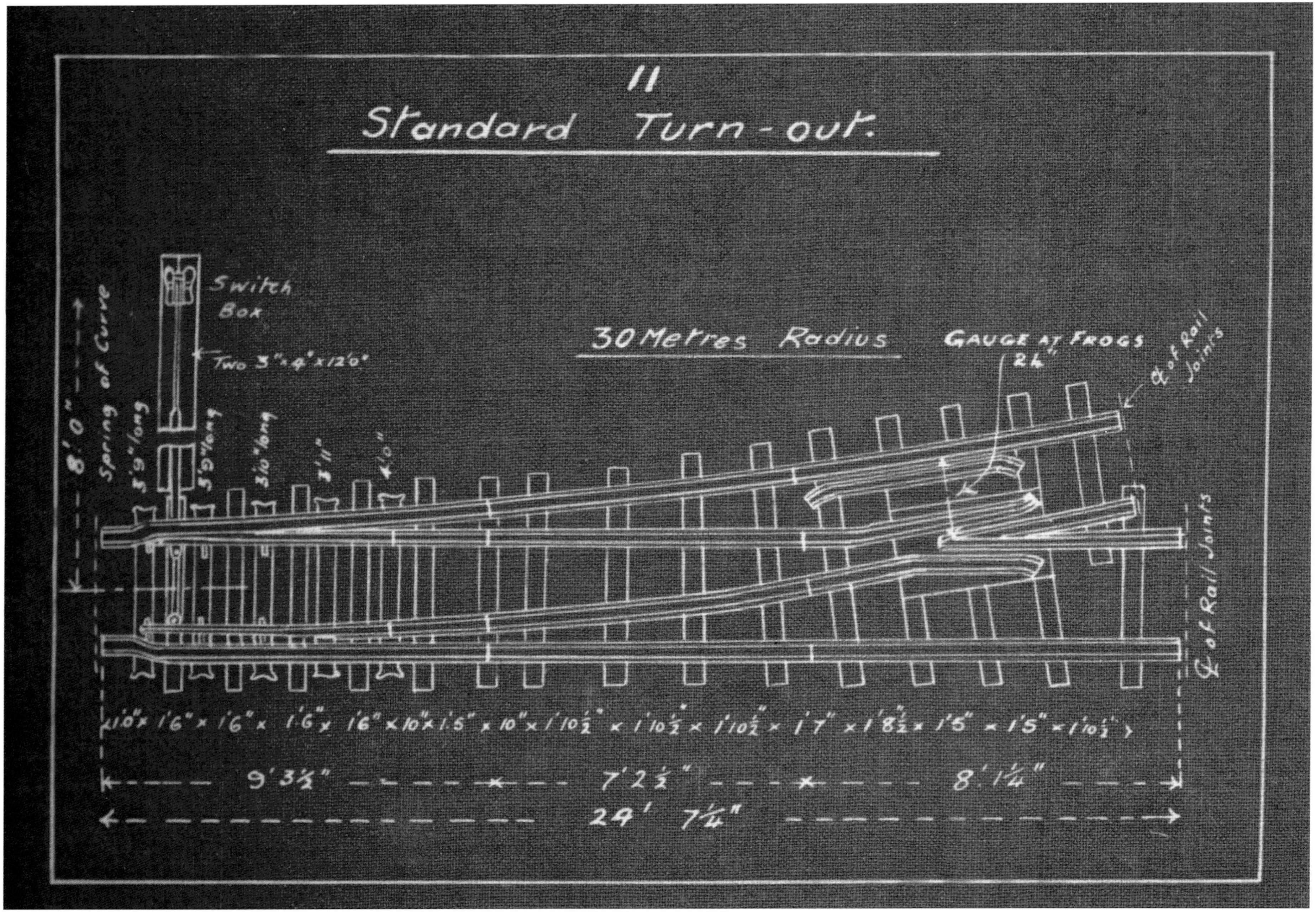

II

Standard Turn-out.

30 Metres Radius

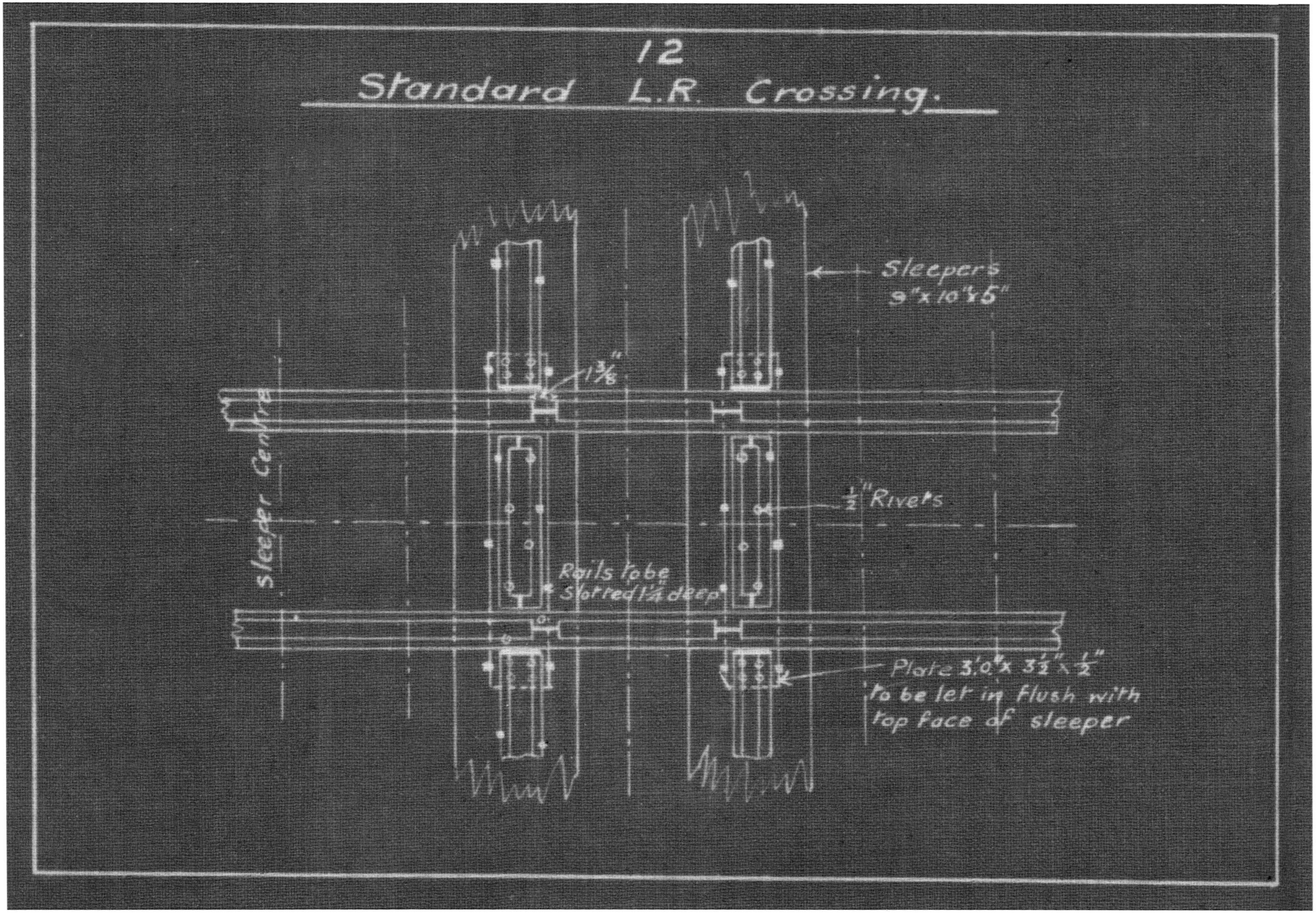
12
Standard L.R. Crossing.
Sleepers
9"x10'x5"
1 3/8"
Sleeper Centre
1/2" Rivets
Rails to be
Slotted 1¼ deep
Plate 3'.0"x 3½"x ½"
to be let in flush with
top face of sleeper

Courtesy Queen's University

13

Standard B.G. Crossing.

Flat Bar 4" x 3/8"

Existing Sleepers.

Timber Packing under 20 lb Rails

12" x 6" Sleeper 14'0" long.

Existing Rail Notched at site Notch 1½" Wide x 1½" deep with edges rounded

Head of Rail planed on running edge to match 20 lbs Rail

Holes for ⅝" Diam Coach Screws

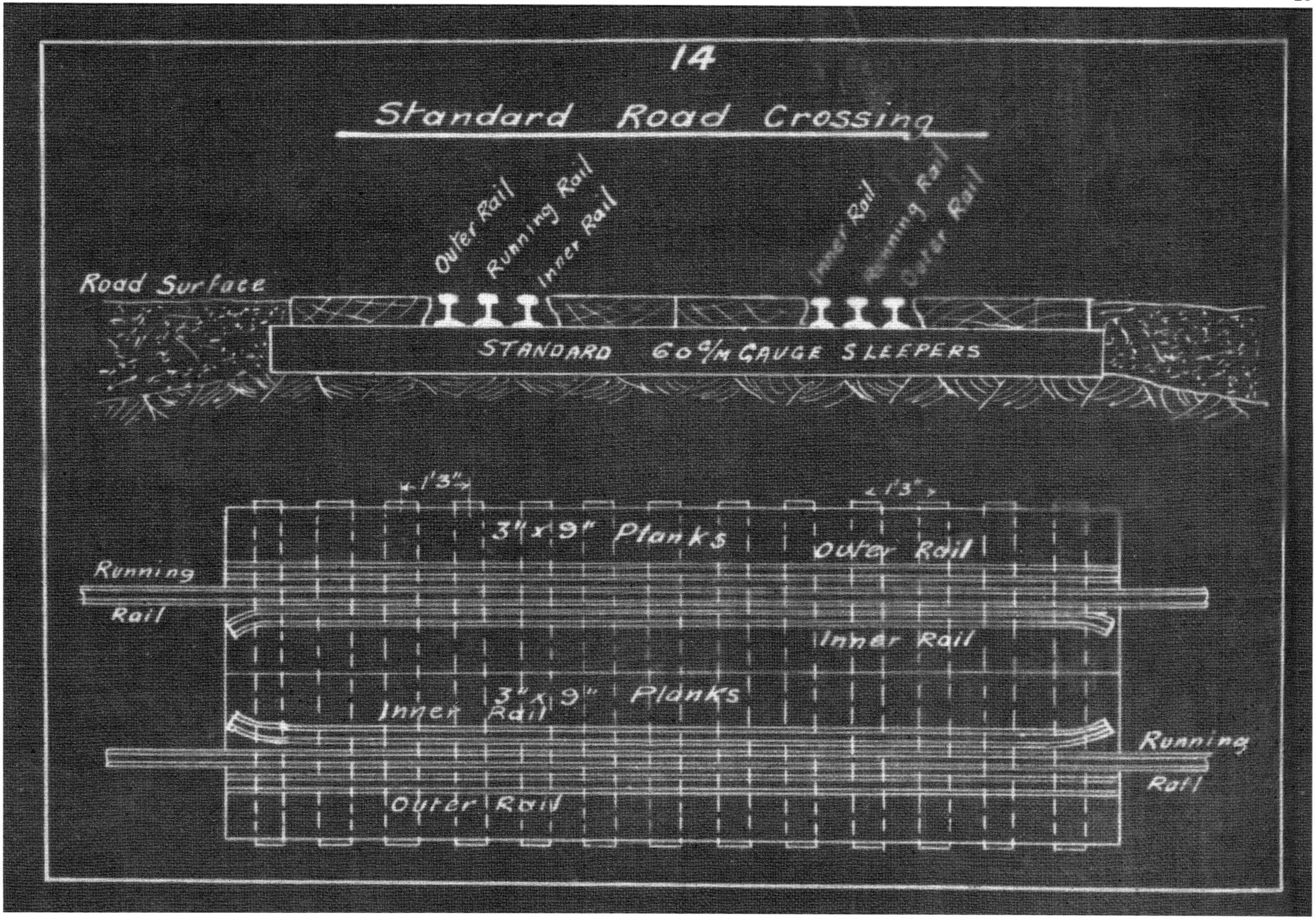

14
Standard Road Crossing
Outer Rail
Running Rail
Inner Rail
Inner Rail
Running Rail
Outer Rail
Road Surface
STANDARD 60c/m GAUGE SLEEPERS
1'3"
1'3"
3"x9" Planks
Outer Rail
Running
Rail
Inner Rail
3"x9" Planks
Inner Rail
Running
Rail
Outer Rail

Courtesy Queen's University

15

Lay-out for Standard Turn-out and Ladder Track.

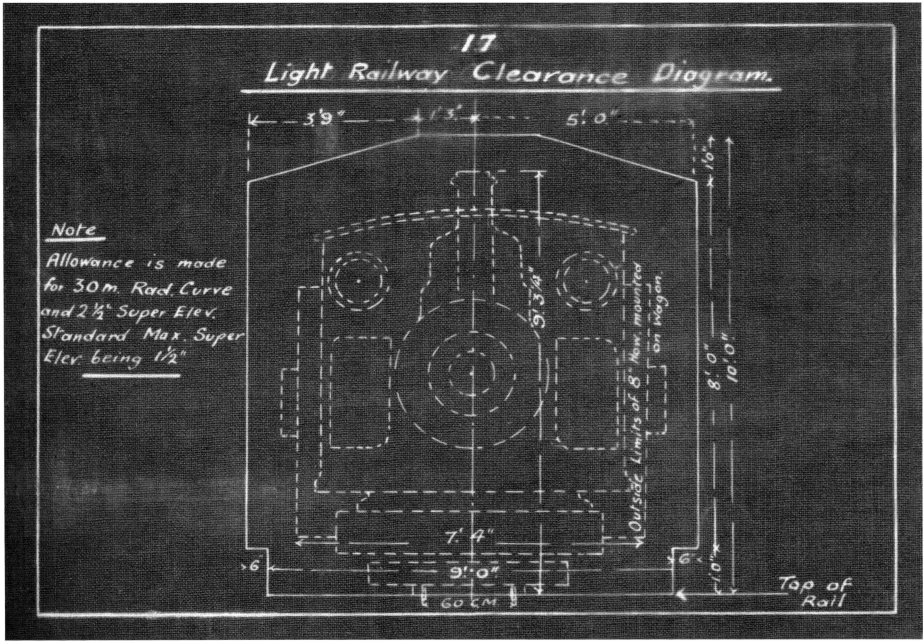

17

Light Railway Clearance Diagram.

Note

Allowance is made for 30 m. Rad. Curve and 2½" Super Elev. Standard Max. Super Elev. being 1½"

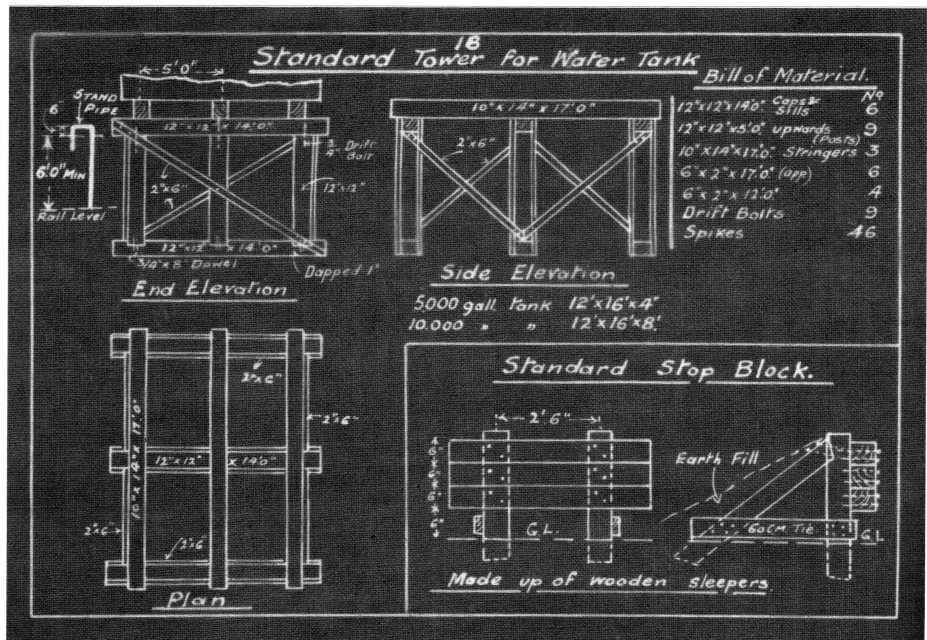

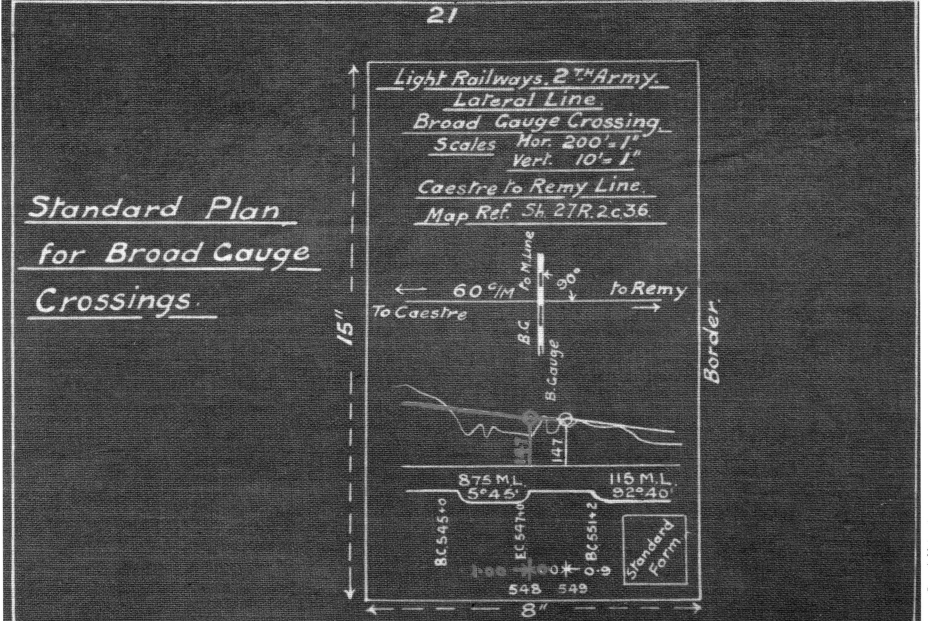

Ditching – 7th March 1918

Straightening and Lifting Gang. A gang of 10 men for straightening, lifting, and packing under sleepers should follow as soon as possible, for convenience using crutch of shovel to pack well under rail ends of sleepers and to a few inches (about 6ins) inside rails. Ganger in charge should see to the straightening, standing well behind and looking along rail and motioning with the arm right or left to the men pulling, and each in turn would, with his lifting bar under the rail and with a lifting, pushing motion, move track accordingly until straight; this should precede packing. See also photograph on page 1.

It was not unusual for German prisoners-of-war to be used on these duties. This is likely to be an RE construction Company at work. Because the RCC units were technically 'non-combatant' the men do not have steel helmets or respirators – though this is surprising in 1918! Perhaps the presence of two young civilian on-lookers means this was an area well behind the lines.

Ballasting and boxing track – 7th March 1918

Ballasting and packing (boxing) of the track and completion of associated works completes the job. The platform here is a standard RE construction – formed from sleepers driven vertically with corrugated iron sheet backing. This was backfilled after timber edging was fixed in place.

Construction train – 7th March 1918

Panels of 20LB per yard steel sleepered track going forward to the railhead. These are loaded on to 'F' class wagons – with the stanchions removed. The men may well be those shown in the photographs on pages 9 and 11. Note that steel helmets and respirators are being carried – mandatory in forward areas.

This train of materials for the Royal Engineers is prepared for enemy attack as it moves closer to the front. The 'duck boards' in the leading wagon, while an essential component of trench construction, were also of use at the railhead, as the photograph on page 8 shows. In this view can be seen small arms for use as crude anti-aircraft guns. There is also evidence of weapons being carried. The locomotive is running 'chimney-first' – the Baldwin 4-6-0T was said to be unstable running bunker-first and turning wyes were incorporated to allow them to be turned at the end of each run. Posed for the cameraman, it is unlikely the men atop the duckboards in the leading wagon would have retained their perch for long once in motion, or particularly, if the wagon derailed.

Untitled

*A lonely stretch of wood sleepered track. The spoil tipped on the low
bank to the right looks like chalk so this scene is probably in the low
chalk hills south of Arras.*

Construction through shell-torn area east of Boesinghe – 7th March 1918

Undulating stretch of straight track bisecting former trenched positions. On the right can be seen a manned block post, part of the operating system. There is utter destruction as far as the eye can see. The condition of the track seen here would have been a major factor with regards to the reputation that the Baldwin 4-6-0T locos built up for rough riding – rocking and swaying alarmingly in such conditions. Preserved examples on much better track are reportedly far better behaved…

Untitled

*Track repair gang, under officer supervision. This
is a RE (RCC) unit at work. The well dressed pair
in the foreground (backs to camera) may well be
the inspecting staff officers' driver and orderly. In
the background, the 60cm tracks are laid directly
over an incoming 'broad gauge' track.*

Canal de l'Yser 'fill' – 7th March 1918

A Simplex 20HP petrol tractor No.103 hauls 4w 'B' class wagon No. R5008 wagon marked "INSPECTION TRUCK" over a newly formed embankment. This has clearly been built up with any available rubble. There is little doubt that the area is, or recently has been, in the range of direct shell fire. Only the trunks of the trees remain. At the right there is a typical Armco corrugated culvert through the formation.

Untitled

Once completed, bridges were subjected to load testing. Here Baldwin 4-6-0T No.789 and train stands on a timber trestle crossing a road. Both British and American crew man the train, which is comprised of heavily loaded class 'E' and 'D' bogie wagons. The locomotive has been fitted with an extended cab roof and a backplate attached to the rear of the bunker. Note the Ford T staff car below the bridge and on the right, a Leyland GS motor lorry.

Given the established look of the embankments on pages 20-21, it may be concluded that this was a former 'broad gauge' formation. The brick-built hut and steps being otherwise an unlikely structure for a 60cm military line laid in wartime. The bridge itself was likely a replacement for a structure damaged or destroyed by enemy action.

Untitled

As page opposite except the test train is now an unidentified 20hp Simplex with two 'D' class wagons. The group with the staff car have been joined by a mounted officer.

Untitled

The same train as seen on page 18, this time on another trestle bridge. Barely visible. lower right, is the inspecting officer's car, also seen in the previous photographs. The rear sheet added to the loco would have been effective at cutting down glare when the firebox door was opened, when running at night.

Untitled

Sometimes, timber alone could not provide the required span. In such cases, steel girders were used, as in this example, constructed by the "3rd Rly Co, R Anglesey RE"– according to the notice on the left hand support. Coming under the heading 'Special Reserve Companies' the 3rd Royal Anglesey Royal Engineers were embodied in August 1914 and in France with the BEF by November that year. The group under the bridge must be members of the aforementioned, plus inspecting officers. Those on the left of the group show a typically varied range of uniform. The single figure on the right, standing behind the bridge is interesting, as he appears to be wearing shorts. The Royal Anglesey RE (Militia) were an 'old' unit which had within it a railway company from pre-1905 days (when it was incorporated in the newly formed Territorial Army). Despite its title, the unit was based in Liverpool.

Untitled

*The same bridge as seen on page 21, with a substantial test train of 'D' class
wagons and two 'E' class. The same open top car is parked along with a motor
cycle and sidecar beneath the structure. Instead of making embankments, as in
earlier examples in the album, this time timber cribbing supports the track above
the terrain. Given its span, possibly this is the "demolished timber viaduct, 250ft
long, reconstructed and available for traffic in 48 hours" mentioned on page 2.
The troops in the full brimmed 'Montana' hats are American.*

Troop train drawn by petrol electric locomotive crossing trestle bridge

A Dick, Kerr 4w PE loco hauling three 'D' class bogies loaded with troops on a curved embankment and trestle. Crews preferred running these tractors cab first, as it gave a better view of the way ahead. The trestle is a typical RE design – single X-braced wooden trestle bents and spans composed of wooden beams. The diagonal bracing from the front of the centre pier to the tops of the two side piers was optional. See text on page 10 and drawings on page 15.

CHAPTER TWO
SUPPLYING THE FRONT

Development: Traffic Volume: Operating: Description of Traffic: Light Railways Left Behind

HE DEVELOPMENT OF TRAFFIC handled by light railways was very remarkable. In January 1917, the traffic averaged 10,325 tons weekly, whereas, in September, this figure had risen to an average of 210,808 tons per week. The average haul was between four and five miles. Of course, this huge increase of traffic could only be handled by a large increase in rolling-stock, the actual figures of which are set out below.

	1917	1918
March quarter	228,334	2,468,629
June quarter	831,967	1,486,188
September quarter	2,276,749	1,889,779
December quarter	2,401,314	997,662
Total	5,738,364	6,831,198

During the period of the battles of Passchendaele and Cambrai (August to November), ammunition carried by light railways averaged over 50,000 tons per week, whilst, during September, 1917, the light railways carried an average weekly traffic of 208,600 men. As a result of the thorough organisation of light railway working, the operating results improved considerably. In March, 1917, the turn-round of wagons averaged 1·7 days, whereas, from August to December, the turn-round averaged 0·9 days. The ton-mile per route-mile per day, which, in February 1917, averaged 56, rose to 225, this indicating an increase in efficiency of 300 per cent. It might also be noted that the ton-miles per locomotive equivalent in traffic averaged 140 per day in February, 1917, whereas this figure worked out to 343 in September, 1917.

TRAFFIC VOLUME

During the year 1918, light railways experienced several great changes of fortune. Just prior to the enemy offensive in March, record traffic was being handled, but, in the course of the enemy advance, a large portion of the light railway network, together with a considerable amount of rolling-stock and power, were lost. This imposed a great strain

1917				
	January 1	March 31	June 30	September 30
Locomotives	68	126	371	650
Tractors	27	68	262	360
Wagons	560	1,306	2,937	4,403

on the organisation, and necessitated an almost entire re-arrangement of the system, though little could be done until a position of stability was established on the Front. The re-organisation of existing facilities and construction of new lines was undertaken in June and, after the opening of the Allied counter-offensive, large mileages of light railway were uncovered in the extensive retreat of the enemy. These lines were immediately exploited in following up the advance. In between March 21 and the end of April, 1918, the route-mileage operated dropped from 920 to 360, but increased by October to 800 miles.

As the Allied Armies continued to advance across Belgium, the light railway system was left far behind, and traffic fell rapidly. In fact, the decrease was so pronounced that, in the quarter ending December, 1918, very little more traffic was handled than in the June quarter of 1917, although the mileage was much more extensive. The following figures indicate the tonnage carried in quarterly

periods during 1917 and 1918, and it will be seen that during 1917 and up to March 1918, the traffic shows a remarkable development. During the second half of 1918, it might be mentioned, the average haul increased considerably with the result that the total ton-miles for 1918 were one and a half times greater than for 1917.

It will thus be seen that the 1918 traffic was over a million tons in excess of the 1917 figures, and this would undoubtedly have been much greater but for the heavy fall occasioned by the great loss of track in the enemy offensive. Traffic increased rapidly after the opening of the Allied counter-offensive and was maintained until the armies advanced beyond the limits of the light-railway systems.

In spite of the difficulties under which light railway working was conducted during 1918, the operating results markedly improved during the year. Whilst the loaded wagon-miles in January averaged 57·5 per power unit in traffic per day, this figure increased to 100·6 in August. Locomotives in steam, moreover, which averaged 28·3 miles per day in January, averaged 41·8 miles per day in July, whilst tractors in traffic increased their work from 26·4 miles per day to 33·8 in July.

The Railway Gazette, September 21st, 1920

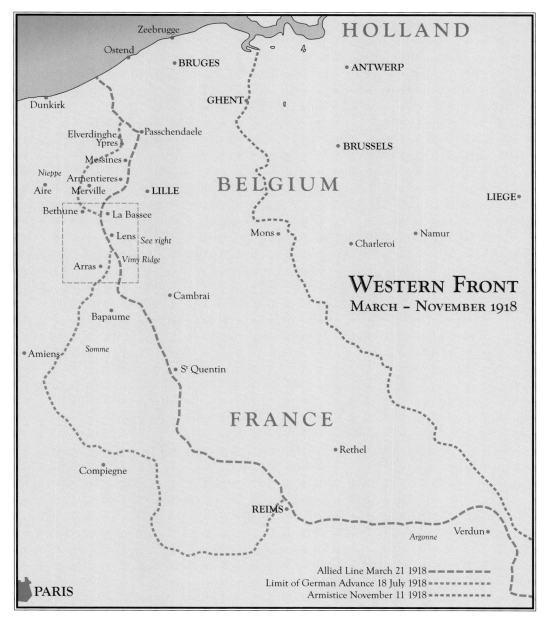

WESTERN FRONT
MARCH – NOVEMBER 1918

Allied Line March 21 1918 — — — — —
Limit of German Advance 18 July 1918 ············
Armistice November 11 1918 ·-·-·-·-·-

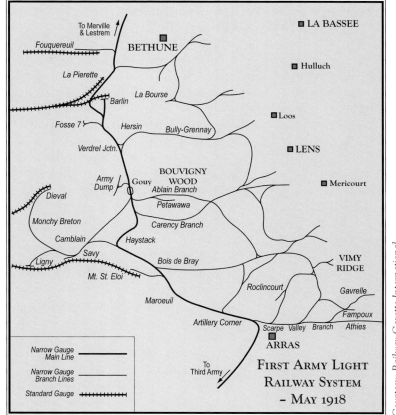

Courtesy: Railway Gazette International

Narrow Gauge
Main Line —————

Narrow Gauge
Branch Lines ————

Standard Gauge ┼┼┼┼┼┼┼

FIRST ARMY LIGHT
RAILWAY SYSTEM
– MAY 1918

Above: The First Army light railway system consisted of a main line running roughly north to south from Bethune to Maroeuil, 4 miles west of Arras, numerous branch lines running from various points on this main line eastwards towards our front-line-infantry positions, and an 'escape' line running westwards from the southern end of the main line back to Savy, Ligny and Dieval, all on the standard gauge railway. The whole of the line was made up of single track, with the exception of a short stretch of main line at Gouy, where separate 'up' and 'down' roads had been laid, and, of course, at stations and passing places. The portion of main line at the southern end, from Bray Loop to Artillery Corner, was at one time worked by the Third Army, but was taken over from them by the First Army in April, 1917. See text starting page 44 for a description of how this was operated.

The Railway Gazette, September 21st, 1920

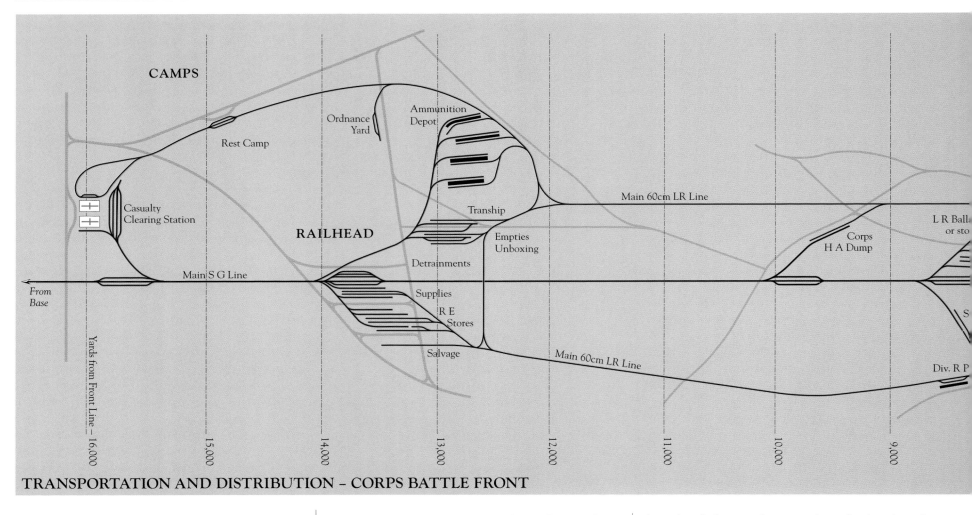

TRANSPORTATION AND DISTRIBUTION – CORPS BATTLE FRONT

Although the above diagram (re-drawn from a contemporary document) is 'idealised' it is likely that it was based on a real situation. While no reference was made to the number of units being supported on the Front Line, a Corps would have under command at least two Divisions (occasionally three), each of which would command three Brigades, in turn each commanding three or four Battalions of infantry. At Divisional level there would be additional troops (Artillery, Engineers, Pioneers etc) under the direct command of the Divisional commander. These were allocated as appropriate to the tasks in hand.

Re-supply was on a 'commodity' basis – ammunition being handled separately to everything else directly to the dumps. The Royal Engineers (RE) have their own stores Depot and this would include everything required for maintaining the system, including all trench materials.

The standard gauge line was, possibly, an existing section, adapted by the RE for military purposes. It would

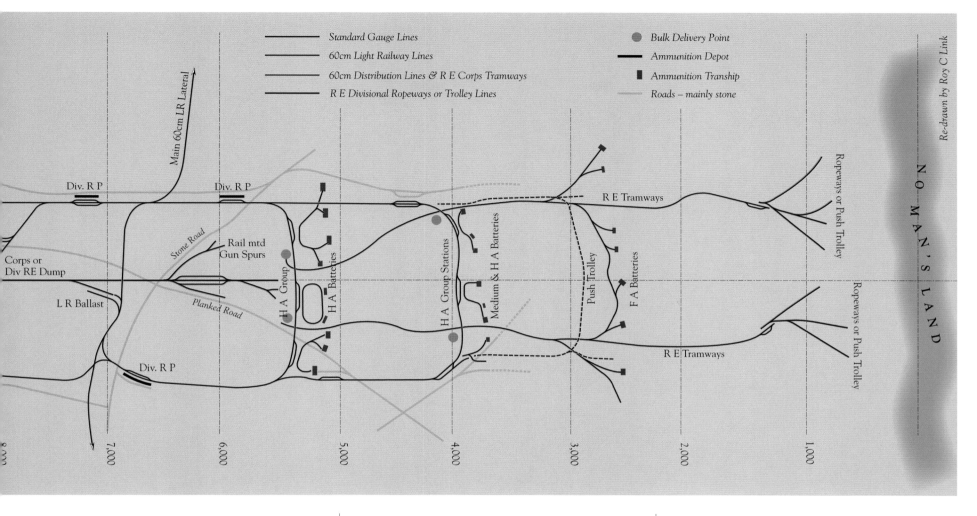

Legend:
- Standard Gauge Lines
- 60cm Light Railway Lines
- 60cm Distribution Lines & R E Corps Tramways
- R E Divisional Ropeways or Trolley Lines
- Bulk Delivery Point
- Ammunition Depot
- Ammunition Tranship
- Roads – mainly stone

Re-drawn by Roy C Link

N O M A N ' S L A N D

Main 60cm LR Lateral

Div. R P
Div. R P
Div. R P

Corps or Div RE Dump

L R Ballast

Stone Road

Planked Road

Rail mtd Gun Spurs

H A Group

H A Batteries

H A Group Stations

Medium & H A Batteries

Push Trolley

F A Batteries

R E Tramways

R E Tramways

Ropeways or Push Trolley

Ropeways or Push Trolley

7,000 6,000 5,000 4,000 3,000 2,000 1,000

have been capable of accepting heavy trains – essential for supply in bulk. In addition, it allowed large rail-mounted guns to approach the front – though this was hazardous as steam locos were required for their movement. In use, they would be brought up, engage the target, fire a few salvoes and promptly retreat, to a safe distance.

The 60cm system was primarily concerned with distribution, in particular supplies to the Heavy Artillery (HA), Medium Artillery and Field Artillery (FA) batteries close to the front. As may be noted, the layout is such that the 4-6-0T Hunslet and Baldwin locomotives could be turned easily as there are a number of 'wye' formations.

Steam would give way to IC power beyond the main 60cm lateral. Light tractors eventually gave way to push trolleys, monorails or ropeways as the front came closer. These were essential in order to provide flexibility if circumstances demanded. Later, in 1918, a second 60cm lateral was considered at the 12,000 yard position – see page 78.

OPERATING – A PERSONAL RECOLLECTION

The headquarters of the operating company with which I was connected were situated at Maroeuil, near Arras, and when I arrived there the town was very badly damaged. The Chemin-de-fer du Nord standard gauge station was damaged very considerably, and the standard gauge railhead had, therefore, been moved back a couple of miles to Mont St. Eloi. A few days prior to my arrival a shell had twisted the substantial water column on the station platform like so much scrap iron. The personnel of the operating-company at Maroeuil lived in wooden huts, sandbagged a portion of the way up as a protection against shrapnel and shell fragments. Dug-outs were available for shelter in the event of enemy shelling or air raids. The company's locomotive sheds and wagon shops were at Maroeuil, while the district traffic control office was located at Artillery Corner, near the village of Anzin, and midway between Maroeuil and Arras. At that time our front line positions were located roughly 4 miles east of Arras. It was at Artillery Corner that I made my home. All of us there lived in dug-outs constructed in the hillside, at the foot of which the River Scarpe placidly flowed eastwards, through Arras and towards the German lines. Behind us were the big guns, and in front the field guns.

TRAFFIC CONTROL

For the district traffic control office we had a roomy dug-out built in the hillside. Down the centre of the place ran a plain wooden table, at which sat the controllers and clerks. Along one wall was fixed the control board – a huge board painted black, with white grooves running along it to represent the railway system over which we worked, and with the name of each station, siding, dump, etc, painted in white letters in its proper place (above). Wire clips, to which a wooden tag was affixed, with the number of the engine painted thereon, were moved along the grooves on the board to coincide with the actual movements outside, as advised to district control over the telephone by the various outside control posts. Into these

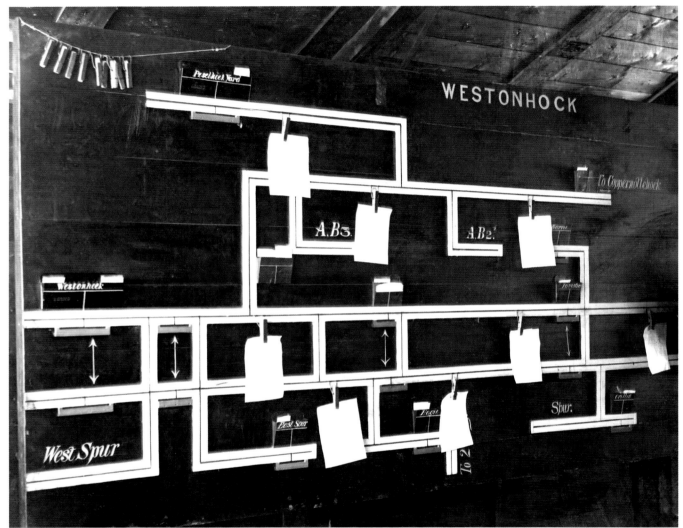

Central control, Vox Vrie – 7th March 1918
Movement control board, showing how painted counters were hung on simple cup hooks bearing numbers or letters – corresponding to stock at the various locations.

Page opposite: District control board showing how lines were represented with slotted wooden rails. The details of the trains are typed on sheets of paper, held by clothes pegs and a wire runner, so they could be slid along as they progressed on their journey.

Forward Area Sub Control Westonhoek – 7th March 1918
Well protected with sandbags and surrounded by the clutter of Army life – note the broom for keeping everywhere clean!

Arras

"As many as 35 men were conveyed in an ordinary narrow gauge open wagon, and eight wagons usually formed a train load in this district." Dick, Kerr 4w PE pauses with a train of 'E' and 'D' class bogie wagons carrying Scottish troops away from the frontline.

clips were placed specially printed slips of paper – one for each wagon – giving details as to wagon number, contents and station from and to. The information given on these slips was also transferred to the wagon books daily, and it was thus possible to tell at a glance what traffic had been dealt with on any particular date.

The staff in the district control office worked in three shifts of eight hours each. On each shift were one sergeant in charge, two traffic controllers, two clerks and one telephone operator. The district went forward – that is, in an easterly direction – from Artillery Corner, through St Nicholas just north of Arras, to Rodincourt, and so on to the foot of the Vimy Ridge, with a branch going off at St Nicholas along the Scarpe Valley to Athies and Fampoux. Behind, it extended to Bois-de-Bray, from which point another operating company took over the traffic. Altogether

there were about 20 miles of track, with extensive sidings at Artillery Corner and Maroeuil. Something like 16 outside control posts at different points on the line were staffed by us, and reported by telephone to the district control office at Artillery Corner the movements of all trains in their sections. Almost all of these control posts were located in dug-outs, varying in depth from 4 to 20ft.

One of these dug-outs – that at Plateau, beyond

Roclincourt, and in sight of the enemy front line – in addition to serving as the light railway control post, also at times accommodated wounded walking cases from the trenches. During my stay in the district we inaugurated a system whereby the outside control staffs were given alternate spells of duty in the more advanced posts and those located further behind the front. The staff in the district control office were specially skilled, and remained on duty there throughout.

TRAFFIC WORKING INCIDENTS

In the rear areas behind Artillery Corner traffic was worked by steam locomotives, and on the forward lines beyond that point by 20 and 40HP petrol and petrol-electric tractors. About 1,000 tons of traffic was handled every 24 hours, consisting principally of ammunition, personnel, guns, rations, engineering material, poison gas cylinders, salvage and ballast for railway and road construction. Whatever happened, the batteries served by the light railway had, at all costs, to be fed. Their appetite, too, was phenomenal.

We had some rather exciting times running up shells for the guns at night. Looking backwards, it appears miraculous how sometimes the light railway trains managed to get through at all, for, often enough, enemy shells landed all around, on more than one occasion half burying the train crew in flying debris. Our casualties were remarkably light: on one occasion a shell landed clean in the middle of a train of six wagons, smashing two of them to bits. The driver of the tractor hauling the train and the guard riding on the rear wagon, escaping unhurt, coolly set to and cleared the line, re-railed the tractor, which had come off the road, and carried on with the remaining four sound trucks.

Working in the dark on a derailment, not daring to show a light, and with enemy shells landing in the neighbourhood, and our own batteries firing right under our nose, was not exactly a picnic. It frequently happened that, after working on a derailed tractor or wagon for some time, it was found impossible to re-rail it before daylight, and so it had to wait until the following night, when a party would set off and finish the job, wondering the whole time whether the enemy would have noticed the tractor or wagon lying there during the day, and open up fire on the assumption that a party would go out at night to get the derailed vehicle on the line again.

DESCRIPTION OF TRAFFIC

During my stay at Artillery Corner many thousands of troops were carried to and from the front. As many as 35 men were conveyed in an ordinary narrow gauge open wagon, and eight wagons usually formed a train load in this district. For the conveyance of artillery special steel gun bogies were utilised, and a train load of these would be made up of four, five or six loaded bogies, according to the size of the guns. The batteries invariably provided escorts to travel with each gun, and also labour to assist in loading and unloading. In times of stress the narrow gauge lines performed much useful work in conveying the guns back to a place of safety.

The ration traffic dealt with in the district travelled principally over the Scarpe Valley line towards Athies and Fampoux, skirting en route the northern suburbs of Arras. This line was under direct observation from enemy balloons, and could only be worked at night. Four ration trains were loaded up daily at Maroeuil and Mont St Eloi, and were hauled thence to Artillery Corner yard by steam locomotives. As soon as darkness fell, petrol locomotives conveyed the trains to their destination, which at one point was within rifle and machine gun range of the enemy line. On arrival there the wagons were unloaded by the infantry, and the empties hauled back to Artillery Corner or used for bringing troops back to rest billets.

The engineering material handled consisted principally of 'elephant iron' wire netting, and cement for the construction of dug-outs and 'pill boxes,' iron stakes, barbed wire and defence timber, and concrete slabs. All this was important traffic, but like everything else it had to give preference at times to ammunition.

The conveyance of loaded poison gas cylinders formed an interesting but rather dangerous part of the work performed by the light railways, and thousands of train loads of deadly gas were worked up to the liberating points by their aid. Much salvaged material, also, was brought down from the front by light railway to salvage dumps at standard gauge railheads, and considerable economies thereby effected.

A TRAFFIC EXCHANGE

At Artillery Corner traffic was exchanged with the Third Army, who held the adjoining portion of the front. The junction with that Army system was situated about half a mile east of Artillery Corner, the line branching off in a southerly direction, skirting the western portion of Arras and running thence through Dainville to Simencourt. A most efficient telephone system enabled us to keep in touch with the Third Army controls in regard to traffic on and off that line.

Whilst on the subject of telephonic communication, mention should be made of the excellent work performed by the Signal Section of the Royal Engineers in this and other districts. To keep traffic moving, and so keep the guns going, and the front line positions supplied with men and material, it was at all times absolutely essential that telephonic communication from the district control office to the outside controls should be maintained. Time and again our telephone lines were severed by hostile shell fire and, no matter at what hour of the day or night this happened, the signal staff set out and made good the damage. How hazardous was their work may readily be realised.

The men at Artillery Corner, like so many other light railway units on detachment, away from company headquarters, were unfortunate by reason of the lack of facilities for amusement and recreation in the off hours at their disposal. Notwithstanding this, and the natural tendency to melancholia inseparable from dug-out life, they remained wonderfully cheerful. All were old railwaymen, and over occasional copies of the home railway publications they had many interesting discussions. Never once did they lose their interest in home railway affairs, and always were they eager for 'shop talk.' Out in the control posts on the line there was usually a tattered copy of some railway publication or other lying about, and on the walls photographs galore of locomotives, stations and so on, clipped from magazines from time to time.

ARMING OF THE RAILWAY OPERATING TROOPS

In view of the possibility of a sudden enemy break-through, the whole of the personnel of the First Army Light Railways were early in 1918 provided with rifles and bayonets, and opportunity taken to give them practice on the range. In connection with the possibility of a German break-through, our plans for the evacuation of the light railway locomotives and rolling-stock were all cut and dried, and every officer and senior non-commissioned officer was given an outline of the form this evacuation would take, and more definite instructions as to his own particular part in the operation. Had the Germans succeeded in breaking through the First Army positions in 1918, the chances are they would have secured little, if any, light railway rolling-stock; all stock would have been withdrawn behind our retiring troops, the lines blown up in vital places, and such works on the line as pumping stations, water tanks, locomotive sheds and the like rendered useless before the enemy arrived.

GOUY MARSHALLING YARDS

At Gouy, some miles north of Artillery Comer, were situated the First Army Light Railway central marshalling yards. Here was the only stretch of double track on the whole of the main line in the Army area, and something like 800 loaded wagons per day were dealt within the yards

in addition to empties, traffic for all parts of the system passing through. The loaded wagons were sorted at Gouy and assembled in train loads for their various destinations. The yard was of the usual flat type; no gravitational yards existed, so far as I could learn, anywhere on the British light railways in France. It consisted of two portions – an 'up' and a 'down' yard – the former dealing principally with traffic going towards the Front, and the latter with the return traffic. In the 'up' yard' there were five roads, each capable of accommodating about 30 wagons; and in the 'down' yard four slightly shorter lines. Empties were collected into train loads in the 'down' yard, and any slight damages made good on the spot by the wagon repair staff, serious damages being left to the wagon shop staff at Barlin, 5 miles to the north, where the headquarters of the First Army Light Railways were situated. Shunting operations were performed by the ordinary train engines.

All kinds of traffic passed through Gouy and, as it was no infrequent occurrence for a stray enemy aeroplane to come over in the daytime, the yards were invariably kept as free from traffic as possible. Often at busy times, however, there would be as many as 80 or 100 wagons of high-explosive shells standing in the 'up' sidings at the same time waiting engine-power to lift them. A very large troop movement in the district or the working of trains of gas cylinders up to the front in preparation for a big attack, which drew the locomotives away from their ordinary work, usually resulted in congestion at Gouy. We were most fortunate, however, as regards our freedom from enemy shell fire. If a shell from the enemy had dropped on our yard at times of pressure, there would have been very little left of Gouy. Only once, however, did a shell land anywhere in the immediate

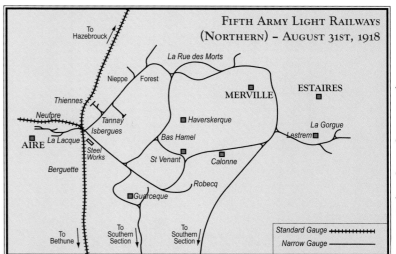

Courtesy: Railway Gazette International

vicinity, and this demolished a well which had been sunk in the 'down' yard to obtain water for the locomotives, smashing up in addition the pump-house alongside. It always struck me as an inexplicable thing why the enemy did not shell the Gouy yards in earnest, for he must have known quite well of their existence. In addition to the observation aeroplanes which came over, it was possible on a clear day to see his balloons, and from them he could not have failed to watch the movements of trains in and out.

CAMOUFLAGE

In connection with enemy observation from the air, and consequent shelling, an interesting occurrence arose at Bois-de-Bray, a little to the south of Gouy. The enemy frequently used to shell a duckboard track there leading to an old, disused infantry camp, and we often wondered at his partiality for this target, for the light railway a short distance away was rarely hit. Eventually a photograph came into our possession taken by an enemy airman, and on the explanatory notes alongside being examined, it was discovered that the duckboard track in question had been mistaken by the German 'intelligence' staff for an 'important light railway.' No reference was made on the map to the light railway proper.

LIGHT RAILWAY REORGANISATION

On the Fifth Army being reorganised after the retirement on the Amiens front in the spring of 1918, it took over the portion of Front lying between Bethune and Armentieres, and the light railway system was quickly developed in this area. The northern section, with which the writer was connected, made its headquarters at La Lacque, about 2 miles north-west of Berguette. As shown on page 49, the light railway system then consisted of a main north to south line running from La Lacque to Bethune, with a connection at its southern end with the First Army system, and branch lines running eastwards from this lateral towards the infantry positions. At the outset the northern section simply served an engineering dump on the standard gauge at La Lacque and an ammunition dump further west at Neufpre, which had also standard gauge connection, and which was situated on the outskirts of the town of Aire-sur-le-Lys. The last portion of track between Neufpre and Aire was only suitable for the passage of trucks pushed by hand, and was used for the transport of material to a bridging school of the Royal Engineers on the Lys Canal, and an RE electric power-station. The engineering dump at La Lacque was formed on what had been the site of the central light railway workshops. These shops were enormous places, full of costly machinery of every description for the repair of steam and petrol locomotives, and rolling-stock and, when first laid down, our front line infantry positions were 20 miles distant. When the enemy made his advance there in the spring of 1918 the place was evacuated, and the shops transferred to a safer site at Beaurainville, between Hesdin and Etaples. The enemy shelled the La Lacque workshops at the time of his advance, but practically the whole of the shops and their contents were safely transferred to Beaurainville.

About a couple of miles to the south-east of La Lacque were situated the Isbergues steel works, run by the French, the second largest works of its kind in the country. These works continued to employ many hands, and turned out large quantities of steel – approximately one-sixth of their pre-war output – despite daily enemy shelling and bombing.

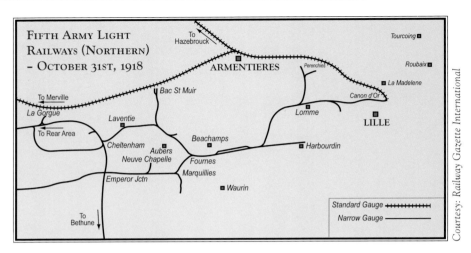

Courtesy: Railway Gazette International

Soon after our arrival at La Lacque we commenced to open up a light railway line running from that point, and passing through Isbergues, to the south-western corner of the Nieppe Forest and through the forest towards Merville. The forest was entered about 2 miles north-east of Isbergues steel works, near the village of Tannay. Just prior to entering the forest a branch left the main line and went to Thiennes, on the Hazebrouck-Isbergues standard gauge line. At Thiennes there was at first simply an RAMC casualty clearing station and an engineering dump but, as time went on, the place was opened out as a standard gauge railhead, and troops and ration traffic were dealt with in considerable quantities.

Although the line from La Lacque to the Nieppe Forest had been in existence some time, little had been done prior to our arrival to develop traffic over it. The ammunition dump at Neufpre and the La Lacque engineering dump were, however, soon opened up seriously; numerous light railway locomotives were put into traffic and a stock of wagons got together, and in a couple of weeks or thereabouts we were carrying well over a thousand tons of traffic daily. There was only one main road through the Nieppe Forest, and alongside this was laid the light railway track. On either side was dense forest with thick, tangled vegetation under the trees, with here and there narrow, winding footpaths leading into the heart of the forest. Along many of these paths the light railway track was laid for the purpose of conveying shells to the batteries concealed in the forest. After passing the 'Street of the Dead,' the light railway line continued to within about a mile of the eastern edge of the forest opposite Merville.

LIGHT RAILWAY
EXTENSION ON ENEMY RETIREMENT

About the middle of August the enemy commenced to retire on this front, and by the beginning of September we had pushed ahead with the narrow gauge line as far as the northern outskirts of Merville, the enemy being then back at Estaires. Until this retirement took place the main road through the forest, along which ran the light railway line, was under direct observation from the enemy balloons and, to conceal to some extent our movements, strips of canvas about 6ft wide were stretched from tree to tree across the road at a height of about 10ft from the ground. As the enemy retired, we quickly pushed the light railway forward,

Westonhoek Marshalling Yard – 7th March 1918

Rakes of 60cm gauge wagons loaded with ammunition for movement to the forward exchange yards and, thence, to the Front itself. On the left are the roofs of standard gauge vans from which the loads came. There are no less than fourteen Baldwin 4-6-0T locomotives in this photograph, many of them in steam, ready to haul the trains. While most of the wagons are class 'D' and 'E' bogies, there are a few 4w class 'B' and, even, an early class 'A'. Lying in the centre foreground is the brake stand off a WDLR wagon.

'Q' Dump yard, Arras – 7th March 1918

Three photographs taken by panning the camera on its tripod and assembled in the album as a triple fold out. The full panorama is shown here, with the individual photos on the next three pages.

and by the beginning of September opened up a line which branched off in a south-easterly direction at Isbergues and, after following the Aire Canal for some 3 miles, proceeded to St Venant, Calonne, Lestrem, the southern outskirts of Merville, and on to La Gorgue. Huge quantities of light railway and road material were rushed up the light railway to keep pace with the retreating enemy, and new traffic controls were constantly established further east as the line grew. After passing Calonne the new line was laid on our old light railway formation and, alongside the new track were the old rails, broken, twisted and torn up by the enemy to hamper our pursuit. On our old lines we came across numerous British wagons which had been captured by the enemy in the spring, many of them quite intact, and these were quickly put into traffic.

The construction of the light railway lines in this district presented a good many engineering difficulties for, although there were practically no gradients, canals, streams and marshy ground abounded. During September 1918, heavy rains seriously interfered with the work of construction and played havoc with newly-ballasted track.

FIFTH ARMY LIGHT RAILWAYS LEFT BEHIND

The retreat of the enemy, begun in August, continued throughout September 1918, and by the end of that month the Fifth Army light railways were left high and dry miles behind the Front, in spite of the efforts of the construction troops to lay steel. As, however, the main ammunition and engineering material dumps, and infantry rest-camps were also situated at an equally great distance from the fighting line, the light railways continued to carry considerable quantities of traffic, including large numbers of troops, up to the end of steel, from which point road transport was employed. New dumps were gradually made further forward but, as our fighting forces were almost daily moving eastward on the heels of the retreating enemy, no permanent dumps could be made, as an advanced dump with light railway connection laid out one day would be miles behind the Front the next. The light railway line by the end of September was being operated as far as Laventie and Fromelles, almost within sight of Lille.

With a haul from standard gauge railhead at La Lacque to end of steel of nearly 20 miles, over a considerable

proportion of newly-laid track, it was somewhat difficult to meet all traffic requirements, particularly as the power and wagon-stock remained the same as had been employed on a small self-contained system with an extreme haul of 8 or 10 miles. At this period train crews worked exceptionally long hours, and if two trips per day per train from standard gauge railhead to end of steel were obtained it was considered good work, especially as labour for loading and unloading trucks was particularly scarce. We had been an exceptionally long way behind the infantry since the beginning of September, but with the capture of Lille on October 18 1918, our light railways were hopelessly out of the fight. The lay-out at the end of October is shown on page 50. Headquarters were then moved up to Lestrem, and steam working introduced as far as Fournes, 6 miles south-west of Lille, while trains drawn by petrol locomotives travelled to Lomme on the town's north-western outskirts.

The Railway Gazette, September 21st, 1920

'Q' Dump Yard, Arras – 7th March 1918

*Left hand photograph of the triptych. Baldwin 4-6-0T locomotives numbers 532, 542 and 747
stand outside a WDLR pattern timber engine shed. Numbers 532 and 542 are early batch locos,
so do not have either water lifters or the characteristic spectacle shields of No.747. Numbers 532
and 542 are without rear lights. The timber buildings were standard Army issue, capable of being
built in multiples of four bays, and similar structures can be glimpsed in other photos.*

'Q' Dump yard, Arras – 7th March 1918

*Central photograph of the triptych. Baldwin No.504 stands with a train of two 'D'
class and three 'E' class wagons. Soldiers in each suggest they are preparing to move
off to load up. The buildings in the background all show clear signs of shell damage.*

'Q' Dump yard, Arras – 7th March 1918

Right hand photograph of the triptych. Just left of centre in the foreground is a door marked 'Petrol Stores' – possibly for IC tractors. In the mid background are standard gauge lines, complete with raised transshipment area and rail mounted crane (page opposite). A line of lorries being unloaded can be glimpsed through the line of trees. Behind them, in the distance, is Arras itself.

Untitled

*An 'open' 40hp Simplex petrol tractor No.2122, with a train
of 'D' class wagons carrying salvaged material being unloaded.
See also pages 72-73. The cylindrical sheel cases are empty – as
are the ammunition boxes, which lack their lids. Anything in
good order could be re-used. Otherwise going for scrap.*

Untitled

Standard gauge wagons being unloaded into 'D' and 'E' class wagons. The nearest 'D' class wagon has a typical assortment of boxed stores. Everything sent to the front was securely boxed in stout wooden packing cases – as it had to withstand loading and unloading many times. The second standard gauge van appears to carry WD ownership markings. A Hudson 'K' class tipper is visible on the extreme right. Note the water tower in the background.

Untitled

A Baldwin 4-6-0T manoeuvres 'F' class wagons alongside standard gauge box vans for loading with supplies. Based on the 'E' class, which had a semi-well design, the 'F' had iron stanchions (detachable) instead of sides or ends. Even so, the total weight both classes could carry was very similar. Note the steam roller load at the left, the Railway Construction Engineers had many such and, by 1918, there was even a dedicated 'Steam Roller Repair Company' deployed in the field. This one, on a standard gauge flat wagon, presumably reached its destination under its own power. The sacks on the third wagon probably contain canvas tentage. The figure on the left is in US Army uniform.

Untitled

An unidentified Hunslet 4-6-0T waits with a train of four 'E' class wagons. The loads are sheeted over, apart from the wagon on the right, which is carrying bales of fodder for army horses. The men are waiting to go forward with the train and are seated on the sheeted wagons as best they can. This must have been a precarious business, even on decent track. The transport of baled animal fodder remained a major task throughout the campaign in France. Nestling among the oil drums (foreground) is a typical 'flimsy' petrol container, the standard method of delivering fuels in forward areas.

Untitled
RE stores dump, behind the lines, being replenished. Much of the material is for trench construction and reinforcement, notably the H section short girders and curved corrugated steel sheets. In the foreground is a stack of coiled wire (not barbed) and, elsewhere, timbers, duck boards etc. The wagon on the right has eight or nine barrels, contents unknown.

Untitled

A similar dump, this one well hidden by a line of trees. Both road and standard gauge railway access is a feature. The train, about to depart on the left of the picture appears to be loaded with RE Stores for trench construction. The load of the static 'D' class wagon and the dump behind consists entirely of artillery shells.

Untitled

*Baldwin 4-6-0T No.799 stands with a rake of four 'D' and 'E' class wagons
loaded with stone ballast. Another train of three wagons, hauled by Baldwin
No.803 waits on another siding – see page opposite.*

Untitled

The ballast for the First Army light railways was obtained from a colliery near Barlin called Fosse 7, the slag heaps being reached by a line of light railway about half a mile in length, leaving the main line between Verdrel and Cairo Junction. The slag, which was loaded into light railway trucks both by hand and by means of a steam navvy manufactured by Ruston & Hornsby Limited, Lincoln, made excellent light railway ballast, and loadings often touched 1,000 tons per day.

Untitled

*Hunslet 4-6-0T No.359 stands with a rake of four 'D' and 'E' class wagons loaded with
supplies. Apart from their army caps, the loco crew could be confused for civilians.
Many exchange yards had their own loco sheds, such as the 'standard' structure
glimpsed on the right. The engine crew are wearing the regulation blue cotton tunics
and trousers (the issue for drivers in peace and war). The soldier/NCO on the left of the
group is probably Royal Field Artillery. While neither of the two front-mounted jacks
supplied with the Hunslet are being carried, there is a re-railing frog/ramp on the cab
roof. Even though this loco numbers from the third batch, it has neither the water lifter
or dome mounted auxiliary steam valve (see page 152). It must be assumed that the
changes were introduced during the batch, and not at the start.*

Train of RE Stores – 7th March 1918

The same train as seen on page 29 – hauled by Baldwin 4-6-0T No.737. Note the camouflaged position just visible on the right, also in the left background, stacks of boxes (ammunition?) sheeted over. The troops are from the 17th (Pioneer) Battalion of the Northumberland Fusiliers – many drawn as volunteers from the North Eastern Railway. Some are armed and prepared to protect themselves and the train if required to. Most interestingly, the man at the left, leaning on the brake-wheel and support has a furled flag under his right arm.

Troop train – 7th March 1918

Baldwin 4-6-OT No.636 with a heavily loaded troop train leaving a standard gauge yard for the front. When necessary, a complete regiment could be moved by the light railways in a matter of hours – one train after another, until the job was done. The wagons are 'D' class, with the sides let down. As the troops have their steel helmets on, it is likely they are en-route for the trenches. However uncomfortable travelling this way undoubtedly was, it was preferable to trudging miles on foot over the shattered landscape, often through mud. In wet weather, their steel helmets and capes would keep off the worst.

Untitled
Hunslet 4-6-0T No.374 paused with a troop train. Without helmets, the men look more relaxed – possibly they are on their way back from the trenches for their fortnight behind the lines. This loco was from the same batch as No.359, on page 64, but has the revised fittings.

Forward exchange yard, Elveringhe – 7th March 1918
Typical scene at a forward exchange yard on the 60cm WDLR lines. Here, steam hauled trains from
the standard gauge exchange terminate, the wagons being broken up into smaller consists. From here
to the Front, internal combustion took over – generally either 20hp or 40hp Simplex petrol tractors.
Almost central in the photo, standing in front of the Simplex tractor, is an officer from a Highland
regiment. The train on the left, hauled by a Baldwin, is taking salvage material back for processing.
Note the end wagon which contains, amongst other items, spent brass shell cases.

Forward exchange yard, Elveringhe – 7th March 1918

Locomotives were serviced and turned around at forward exchange yards, the steam locomotives taking trains of empty wagons back to the standard gauge exchange. Notable in this photograph, just below this caption, is a rare image of a Barclay 0-6-0WT, between the three Baldwins and Hudson Hudswell. Also visible is a train of side-tipping skip wagons. These were class 'K' and supplied in two capacities, either 18 or 27 cubic feet.

Untitled

Two Baldwin 4-6-0T hauled trains, one double headed, wait at a forward exchange yard for their
contents to be moved forwards. A British Westinghouse 4w PE stands ready instead of the more usual
Simplex tractor. The front starting handle is still in place and the two men are leaning on the re-railing
lever. Unlike the Dick, Kerr version, they also had external frame-mounted sandboxes, the leading one
visible here. Many of the soldiers are American, the photo dating from the period when US military
railway troops were familiarising themselves with WDLR equipment and working.

Untitled

Having reached a point close to the forward lines, supplies were often man-handled into carts for final delivery. Clearly visible in this scene (left to right) are wooden boxes – marked bacon, slatted crates of tinned butter, sacks of Lyle's sugar, cases of tinned preserves, sacks of flour – plus baled fodder for horses. On the right are a row of GS horse drawn waggons being loaded for delivery. The GS Waggon was the chief item in an Army Service Corps transport column. The ASC would be drawing rations for the units which it supported. It was at this point that the bulk rations/fodder would be divided up to create balanced rations issued to the units. Note the Military Policeman (light coloured belt), below.

Westonhoek Railhead, trains of salvage off-loading – 7th March 1918

The flow of traffic on the WDLR was by no means all one way. Material shortages of all kinds became more acute as the conflict wore on. By 1918 a well established system of salvage had been established and anything of use was collected and moved to dump areas well behind the lines for re-use. Note the tented camp on the left and crane in the background, just off centre right, for off-loading heavy items.

Salvaged material required a lot of labour and a variety of Allied troops are seen in this image, no doubt all on their two weeks 'rest' from the front line. Much of what is being handled comprises wooden cases for ammunition and 18lb shells. Behind the 'broad gauge' wagons are a line of Baldwin locos, plus a Dick, Kerr PE on a further track and above them, motor lorries can be discerned on a distant road.

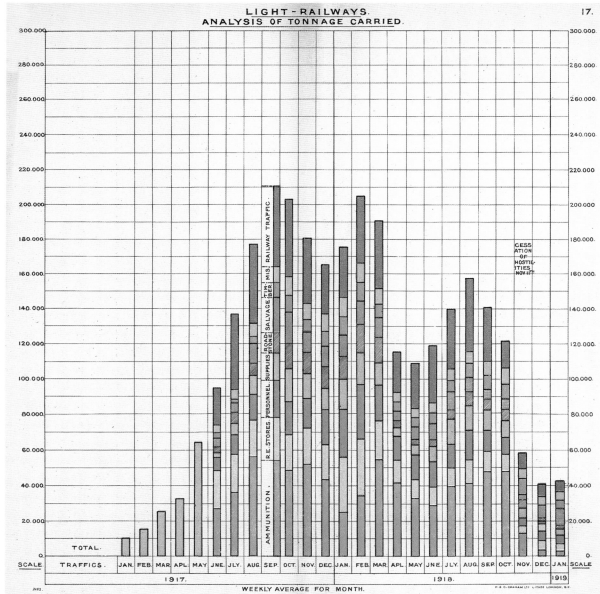

LIGHT-RAILWAYS.
ANALYSIS OF TONNAGE CARRIED.

17.

Left: An official War Department 1919 chart showing a monthly analysis of tonnages carried by the WDLR during the years 1917 and 1918. Comparing the various categories of traffic, from month to month is interesting and the sudden dip, after March 1918, when the final German offensive was launched is very noticeable. After the Armistice in November 1918, traffic dwindled rapidly, with ammunition supplied being greatly reduced, as might be imagined.

Right: Another chart, showing tonnage conveyed weekly, over a similar period, with date notes of significant battles in the conflict. The lower blue line shows ammunition tonnage, the red line general or 'railway' tonnage and the black line represents the total. Solid lines represent the average figure and the dotted lines, actual tonnage.

TRAFFIC CONVEYED

In the work of transport in the area forward of the standard-gauge railheads, the narrow-gauge railways were called upon to convey traffic of a hundred-and-one kinds. The principal traffics may, however, be summarised under the following main heads:

Ammunition, guns, personnel, wounded, rations, engineering stores, poison gas, salvage, and ballast. First and foremost came the ammunition, for the transport of shells to the artillery was the great task of the narrow-gauge railways. The ammunition was, as far as possible, carried to a group of batteries in train loads. Its conveyance was at times a somewhat dangerous task, and the position of the crew of an ammunition train when passing through a heavily-shelled area by no means an enviable one. There was no such thing as halting or turning back when enemy shells commenced to fall in the neighbourhood, for hundreds of lives depended upon the speedy delivery of the train load to the guns. Day and night, in fair weather and in foul, the heavily-laden ammunition trains, with their cargo of high-explosive and gas shells, crept up the narrow-gauge track from the dumps in the rear to the artillery positions and, rarely,

Collection: Colonel David W Ronald

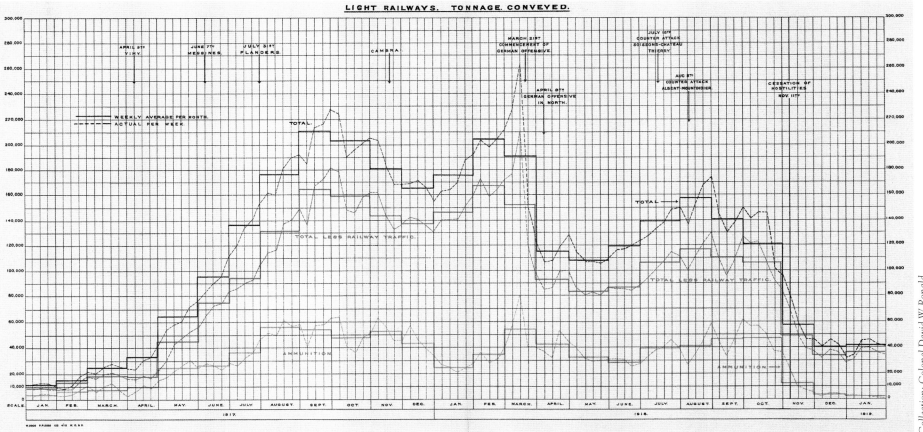

LIGHT RAILWAYS. TONNAGE. CONVEYED.

Collection: Colonel David W Ronald

did they fail to deliver the goods. Many are the stories of hairbreadth escapes from destruction which could be told by the narrow-gauge train crews engaged in the transport of the ammunition, and their determination and bravery knew no limit. The guns, large and small, conveyed over the narrow-gauge railways on wagons specially designed for the purpose, numbered many thousands. In addition to carrying the guns up to their battery positions, the narrow-gauge railways frequently brought them back to the testing ranges which were established in the rear areas, and later returned them to their positions.

Of the wonderful system of salvaging in operation on the Western Front much has been heard. With this economy campaign the narrow-gauge railways were intimately connected. It was their business to haul the salved material of all descriptions from the battlefields to the standard-gauge railheads and, by their aid, large quantities of valuable material were salved and brought down to standard gauge.

There the material was sorted and dispatched in truck loads to the bases at Calais, Boulogne and elsewhere, where it was cleaned and repaired and rendered fit for re-issue. In the war of movement, the narrow-gauge railways conveyed immense quantities of railway and road-making materials up to the forward area and, with their assistance, the task of maintaining touch with the advancing troops was greatly facilitated.

A L Stead (ex Royal Engineers), June 4th, 1920

CHAPTER THREE
FEEDING & MOVING THE GUNS
Ammunition Railheads & Dumps: Systems Connected: Carriage of Guns

HROUGHOUT 1917 LIGHT railways were in process of development and new uses for them were being experimented with. By the beginning of September they were handling a greater or lesser amount of practically everything other than supplies that arrived at the standard gauge railheads. Ammunition for siege and heavy artillery was transferred by the ordnance service ammunition railheads to light railway wagons, either direct or after passing through the railhead depot.[1]

Some batteries were situated near the main lines of light railways; in such case light railway personnel unloaded it at an adjacent group station, so-called because it served a group of batteries, whence it was removed over tram lines provided under corps arrangements and worked by the personnel of the batteries. In other cases batteries were on branch lines or on cross-connections of the light railway system and the ammunition was unloaded at the 'back doors' of the batteries; in such cases there were seldom intermediate tram lines. As a safeguard against interruption of the service near the batteries by the enemy's counter-battery fire, there were artillery refilling points at stations on the light railway main lines, from which ammunition could, if necessary, be drawn by road transport; field artillery ammunition was sometimes delivered by light railways to tramways, but the light railways were extended up to the field artillery zone in only a few cases and were then liable to be interrupted by shell-fire so frequently that

road transport from the light railway ammunition refilling points was the more usual means of transit.

At the forward limit of normal working were stations called trench tramway transfer points. Trench munitions were usually drawn by horse transport from the ammunition refilling points; in some cases the horse transport delivered them to their destination, in other cases it transferred them to tramways at trench tramway transfer points. Occasionally trench munitions were carried by light railway from the ammunition regulating point to a group station, thus reducing the length of haul by horse transport, or to a tramway transfer point, thus eliminating horse transport altogether, but this could be done only when other light railway traffic was slack. The normal route of engineer stores was from a corps park at a standard gauge railhead to a divisional dump and, thence, to the dump of some Field Company RE. When the divisional dump was on a light railway it was filled up from the corps dump by light railway;

beyond the divisional dump stores were taken forward by horse transport or tramway. However, the light railway service was ready to unload engineer stores at whatever station was nearest the place where the stores were to be used. Stone from a standard gauge railhead was delivered at any light railway station, the loading and unloading being done by light railway labour but, as the dumping of stone prevented the use of a station for any other traffic until the stone had been moved it was usual to provide special sidings for road material. These could be quickly laid to places where much stone was needed and taken up again when the work for which the stone was needed was completed.

As originally laid out, the light railway system of each Army was an isolated system; the equipment was taken to each system and transfers of rolling stock between systems, and to and from the light railway shops at Berguette, were effected by using the standard gauge railways. The medium artillery zone in all Armies was served by light railways, so that if the systems were connected, it would be possible not only to transfer rolling stock between Armies but also to move 6 and 8inch howitzers and 60-pounder guns direct from positions on the front of one Army to positions on the front of another. It was, therefore, decided in the autumn of 1917 to provide a lateral line running along the front at some 6,000 yards behind the front line trench system to connect up all the systems, and a number of special wagons for the carriage of guns and howitzers were constructed. This lateral was completed about the middle of March 1918. Meanwhile, in the winter of 1917-18, heavy attacks were anticipated in the coming spring; in the event of

---

1 It had been decided earlier in the year that ammunition was not to be stored in the yards of ammunition railheads, but at a depot away from railway premises.

Untitled

In 1917 it was decided that ammunition was not to be stockpiled in the railhead yards but in separate depots. This scene shows a concealed depot, with carefully constructed and well separated 'bunkers' for holding shells prior to moving up to the batteries.

the front being bent back this forward lateral would be liable to interruption. In January 1918, therefore, it was decided to construct another lateral 12,000 yards behind the Front, with certain east and west lines from it running back still further. These rear feeder lines would tap various reserve dumps of ammunition and certain railheads, and also provide refuges for rolling stock in the event of any considerable retirement of the front. This scheme, however, was only in its initial stage when the German offensive started in March.

During the offensive in Flanders in the autumn of 1917 the tonnage brought up by the light railways grew to be more than the tramways could handle; the light railway service was forced to undertake a large proportion of the detailed distribution to batteries over unballasted spurs from 150 to 1,000 yards long, and in extreme forward areas to extend its service over light tramway tracks unsuitable for its motive power and rolling stock. Early in October the Director of Light Railways (DLR) suggested that distribution in detail of what the light railways brought up in bulk might well be treated as a new and separate link in the transport service chain. The Director General of Transportation (DGT) represented that the experience of the Wytschaete-Passchendaele operations showed that in the latest offensives the demands on the light railway service were so heavy that it was no longer possible for it to undertake distribution as well as delivery in bulk; he proposed that, on an offensive front, the tramway service should be enlarged to make it capable of dealing with such distribution in the battle zone as had come to be undertaken by the light railways, and that service should confine itself to delivery to the heavy and medium artillery, and such bulk deliveries of engineer stores and field gun ammunition as it could manage after serving the heavier artillery.

For the next five months the subject was under continuous discussion. The conclusions arrived at early in November were that the recent operations showed that in the forward

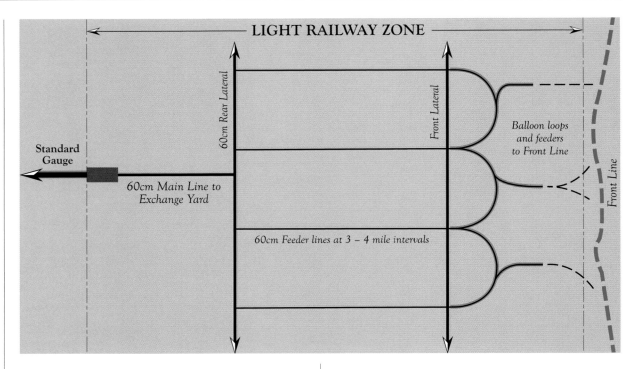

area on offensive fronts the existing means of transport were insufficient to deal with the increased traffic; the system under which stores were delivered in bulk at the standard gauge railheads and then distributed by light railways was an adequate one under normal conditions of trench warfare but, on an offensive front, stores would have to be delivered in bulk further forward, to points within 5,000 yards of the front if possible: the standard gauge railheads could not be advanced with safety nearer than 13,000 yards of the front; light railways must be used for bulk deliveries and some other means of distribution in detail from the light railway groups, stations and refilling, points must be found. A decision somewhat inconsistent with this last conclusion, however, was taken at the same conference, namely, that the DGT should provide and work unballasted light railway

tracks from group stations to groups of heavy and medium batteries and, in the course of subsequent discussions, it appeared that it was intended that this should be the system not only on offensive fronts but everywhere. The whole question had arisen because the light railways were overtaxed by the amount of detailed distribution they were being called upon to do; the DGT pointed out that if distribution to heavy and medium artillery was to be the business of light railways that service would require a large increase in personnel and material.

At the end of December 1917 a circular letter to Armies notified the decision to replace the existing army tramways companies by what were called forward transportation

Continued on page 84…

Loading 15in shells ex normal gauge – 7th March 1918
Note the RFA Gunner, standing next to the open van door has an interesting variant of the 'service cap' incorporating ear protectors. The Chinese labourer on the right with the cap, would be the gang foreman, having sufficient English to act as an intermediary with regards orders etc. See also page 80.

Direct Transshipment From
Normal to 60cm at Swiss Cottage – 7th March 1918

*Above: Panorama comprising three photographs pasted together – that on
the left being attached by a linen strip and folded in to the album. Each of
the three photographs are reproduced, in order, on pages 81, 82 & 83.
Exactly where the location of 'Swiss Cottage' was, is unknown, but is
typical of the confusing names given to key locations on the WDLR – such
as 'Willesden Junction', 'Cheltenham' and 'Artillery Corner' etc.*

*The rake of French standard gauge wagons, containing artillery shells,
are being unloaded into waiting 'D' class wagons. The work is being done
by members of a Chinese 'Labour Battalion' overseen by NCOs and at
least one officer (in boots).*

Loading 15inch Shells – 7th March 1918

*Right: Moving shells from the standard gauge wagons was a task
demanding care and strength. Here, 15inch shells are being loaded into a
'D' class wagon by lowering each one down improvised slides which are
actually corrugated steel sleepers from a 60cm gauge track panel. The
strained ropes and positions of the three men gingerly lowering the shell
down into the 'D' class clearly shows how hard this was. According to an
official document, this class of wagon was allowed to carry a load of up
to eighteen 15inch howitzer shells – a weight of 9·75 tons, the permitted
load being 9 tons 8 cwt – only a little more than the weight of the shells.
To fit these in, a second layer would be required, on top of those seen in
the photograph. Given the quantity of such shells shipped to the front the
physical effort involved by the labourers is truly staggering.*

Direct Transshipment From Normal to 60cm at Swiss Cottage – 7th March 1918

Direct Transshipment From
Normal to 60cm at Swiss Cottage – 7th March 1918
The Lance Corporal on the left has a badge over his rank chevron – third from left is a Lance
Bombardier RFA (white lanyard on left shoulder). The letter V on the wagons indicates the 5th Army
Light Railway Corps. The 'D' class wagon below is being filled with 9·2 inch howitzer shells.

**Direct Transshipment From
Normal to 60cm at Swiss Cottage – 7th March 1918**
*Note the immaculate RHA Sergeant (breeched and booted) on the left.
Some of the Chinese coolies are wearing straw hats to keep off the sun.*

Continued from page 78...

Where a 60cm battery spur or tramway was not available – or when an advance or retreat rendered them useless, shells would be moved by motor lorry, as seen here, despite the churned landscape.

companies, and gave details of the future arrangements. Light railways would normally be laid out on the 'balloon' system, namely, two or more lines running forward from standard gauge railheads with a lateral connection at about the heavy artillery zone and another transversal at about the medium artillery zone.[2]

The light railways would normally deliver stores in bulk at 'bulk delivery points'; these would be of two kinds, namely group stations, whence ammunition for groups of heavy and medium batteries would be distributed by subsidiary distribution lines, and divisional refilling points whence ammunition, engineer stores, stone and other stores would be distributed in detail to places further forward by means of tramways, ropeways or otherwise. The distribution lines from group stations were to be light railway branch lines, usually unballasted, and were to be manned by light railway personnel under the DGT. Tramways and ropeways

distributing beyond other bulk delivery points were to be an engineer service in the province of the Engineer-in-Chief. For their construction, maintenance and operation a number of engineer units were being formed, to work under the Chief Engineers of Armies and to be concentrated in Armies about to undertake active operations. The DGT was to provide the material for the track and the rolling stock for the tramway service and to undertake heavy repairs to the tractors in use on the tramways, but current running repairs to the tractors and rolling stock was to be an engineer service. The use to be made of roads in a

general scheme of distribution had not been overlooked, but the man-power situation was such that the raising of new units for the construction and maintenance of roads in the forward zone was impracticable; roads in front of the DGT line must be dealt with by the pioneer battalions and any RE personnel and labour which might be available. The arrangements notified were to apply primarily to areas of active operations; on defensive sectors light railways and tramways were to continue to operate as before. The name of 'Forward Transportation' proposed for the new organization might lead to some confusion with the organization of the Director General of Transportation, while 'Tramways' as a title was too limited a term to cover all phases of the work which the new organization was to undertake; the title was, therefore, soon changed to 'Foreways.' It was proposed to provide, ultimately, one foreways company per corps; to form a nucleus of skilled personnel the existing nine army tramways companies and one army troops company previously employed almost entirely on tramways were to be drawn upon and each RE field company was to give up four men. To fill the proposed establishments other sources would have to be drawn upon, mainly from home. While the establishments and functions of the new service were being worked out a noticeable alteration was made in the general scheme. The DGT pointed out that, as regards the distribution of ammunition to the medium artillery, hitherto corps had laid the unballasted track up to the gun positions and had undertaken the distribution in detail from the light railway delivery points; the operation of a large number of isolated push-lines was not a practical proposition for the existing light railway organization; if distribution to medium as well as to heavy artillery was to be undertaken by the transportation service a number of supplementary light railway distribution sections with a personnel of about 2,000, exclusive of supervisory and other staff, would be necessary, and the War Office had already said that this additional personnel could not be

2 *The advantage of the balloon system of layout was that all trains could run as a rule in the same direction, thus greatly increasing the capacity of the lines while, in the event of a line being cut by shell-fire or blocked by accident, there remained an alternative route to the place served by the obstructed line.*

Engine & Four Wagons (Shells) – 7th March 1918

Baldwin 4-6-0T No.661 about to depart with four 'D' class wagons loaded with shells. The brakemen are already in place ready to assist. As noted on page 29, these locos were discouraged from running cab forward on 'main lines', but this was not always the case in practice. The relatively intact trees suggest an area as yet unsubjected to intense shell fire. The 'D' class wagons contain 8 inch Howitzer shells, plus round metal containers containing the bagged propellant.

This contemporary illustration captures the scene at a battery during action far better than any photograph.

provided. He recommended a continuance of the existing practice, namely, that light railways should lay and maintain the track up to the heavy artillery and, in the case of the medium artillery, to group stations only, that the new organization should construct, maintain and work spurs from the medium artillery group stations to groups of medium batteries, that the batteries themselves, assisted, if necessary, by the new organization, should lay and work 9LB track used for lines leading up to the individual guns. This proposal was accepted and a General Staff letter to Armies at the end of February laid down that light railways would lay, maintain and operate lines up to group stations in the medium artillery zone, and that foreways would be responsible for distribution from such group stations and in advance of the medium artillery zone. Early in March a General Staff circular memorandum to Armies amplified previous circulars. It laid down that the foreways service was to be an engineer service under a 'Controller of Foreways' at each Army headquarters. The service was to develop and exploit all means of transport of ammunition, rations, stores and ,on occasions, personnel, in the zone in front of that served by light railways. For the time being the foreways service would only be concerned with systems employing mechanical means of traction, but eventually, if and when the manpower situation permitted, the service was to become responsible for roads and tracks in front of the DGT line as well. Light railways were to deliver in bulk to group stations, and to transshipping dumps at places selected with a view to security and facilities for the exchange of trucks and stores. Beyond these points the foreways service would provide facilities for:

(a) Distribution of ammunition to medium batteries in the medium artillery zone.

(b) Distribution to dumps of trench mortar and small arm ammunition, engineer and ordnance stores and rations.

(c) The evacuation of wounded.

(d) The evacuation of salvage.

(e) The transport of personnel if not incompatible with the functions previously enumerated.

The above scheme was never tested in practice; before the end of March the War Office intimated that it was unable to provide the personnel needed to fill the establishments required to work the new service. Then came the German offensive of March and, for two months, the question was dormant.

TRANSPORTATION ON THE WESTERN FRONT
Colonel A M Henniker

Untitled

Soldiers loading 4·5 inch shells directly from 60cm 'D' class wagons into 4·5 inch Howitzer limbers. Compare the buildings and line of trees to those in the background of the photograph on page 53.

Untitled

Baldwin hauled train arriving at a Forward Yard in the First Army Area. There is a great variety of rolling stock present, including some four wheel wagons. Note the class 'E' in the background with upward end extensions – probably for carrying baled animal fodder. Loads visible include boxed ammunition and trench timbers. In the right lower corner there is a primitive home made 'toast-rack' people carrier of some sort. Note also the unusual timber bolster set, in front of the 'B' class 4w wagon.

Untitled

Dick, Kerr 4w petrol electric hauling a pair of 'E' class wagons through the remains of a shelled village in the Lieven-Angres sector (near Lens) en-route to a forward battery. Note how the shells have been stacked over the bogies only, see page 192 for a table of ammunition loads.

Loading to trench tram at battery spur – 7th March 1918

After the shells plus their propellant and fuses were unloaded from the supply train, they were loaded on to push trolleys for delivery to the batteries. These are thought to be 9·2 inch Howitzer shells. Not only was this strenuous manual labour, it was often accomplished under fire from the enemy.

Loading to trench tram at battery spur – 7th March 1918
Note the tarpaulins covering the stacked munitions. A degree of camouflage was essential to avoid enemy reconnaissance aircraft spotting the site. In practice, as noted elsewhere, spotting the 60cm lines from the air proved surprisingly difficult.

Untitled

1 – Stanchions removed, this 'F' class wagon, fitted with side mounted brackets (see page 94) is being prepared to accept a piece of field artillery for transit. Lying either side of the wagon are sturdy girder troughs and a pair of ramps are ready to be set up at the end.

Untitled

2 – One of the girder troughs is lifted up into position on the side bearers. A Hunslet 4-6-0T has been backed up to the assembly, essential to keep it in place while the work is being done. This is because the vertical brake stands have been removed from the bogies. Bogies with horizontal brake mechanisms would solve this – allowing a locomotive to haul the load into place, considerably reducing effort and speeding the process up.

Untitled

3 (above) – The 'F' class prepared to accept the field piece; note the coupler casting has been removed from the bogie at the ramp end. The ends of the ramps were given a secure foundation by three inverted steel channel pads (see page 92) riveted in place. To ease the wheels up on to them, timber wedges were provided.

4 (left) – Close up of the substantial side brackets that hooked over the sides of the 'F' class well. Similar brackets were riveted to inverted U shaped channel for the pairs of supports at the ends. Note that the side troughs do not extend the full length of the wagon.

Untitled

*5 – Ready to receive the load. In the background is a line of Baldwin locomotives and, on the extreme left,
a tantalising glimpse of a French Pechot-Bourdon 0-4-4-0T. The Hunslet is from one of the later batches,
distinguished by the water lifter hose brackets on the back of the bunker and protected rear spectacle glasses.
Note that the coupler link retainer remains on its chain – though the coupler body has been removed.*

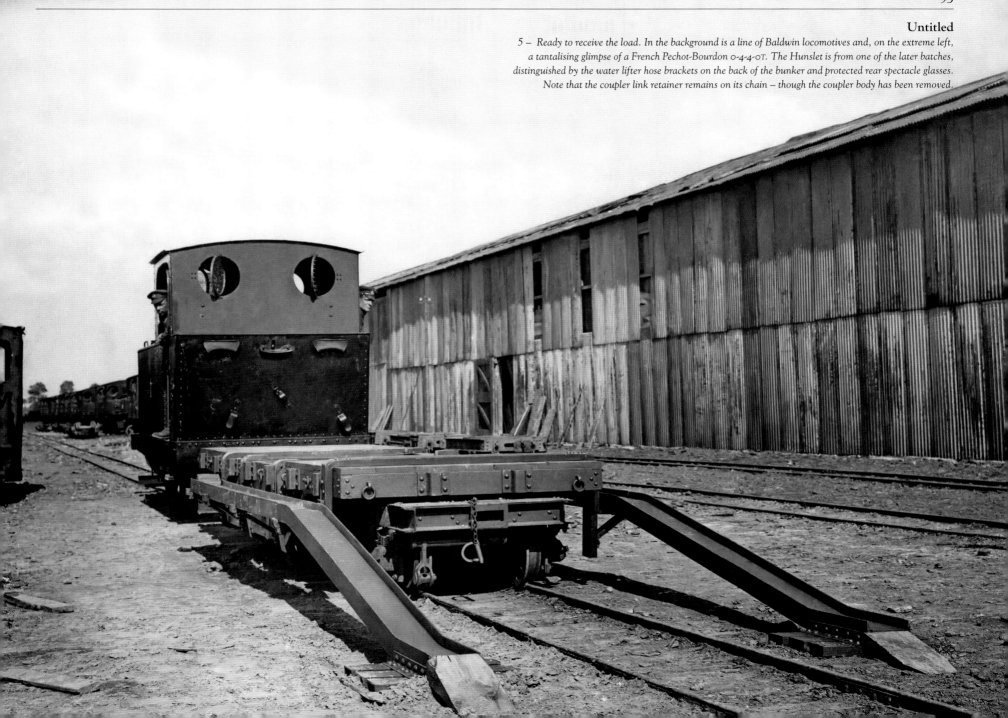

Untitled

*6 – A group of eight soldiers, four per side, haul the artillery piece up
on to the wagon. The rope position acts as a lever on the wheel rim,
allowing more control over the movement of a very heavy object.*

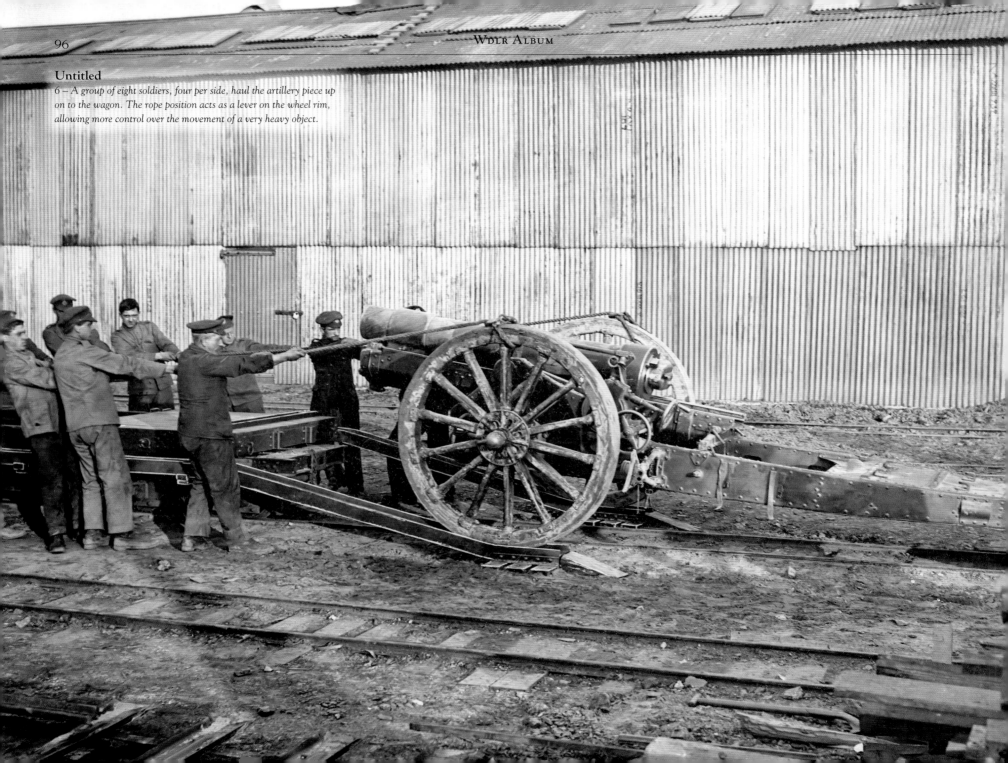

7 – Once the artillery piece is safely on the wagon, the pair of ramps are placed either side, ready for the off-loading procedure on arrival at the delivery point.

Untitled

8 – Finally, the limber is placed on the wagon behind the gun and the whole made ready for transportation. As yet, neither are chained or roped down, essential for their journey over often rough track.

The artillery piece is a 6 inch 26cwt howitzer, developed in 1915 to replace earlier, inadequate types in the light of experience against German artillery. Entering service late in 1915, the new howitzer became a pivotal weapon in Britain's armoury. Some 3633 pieces had been produced by the end of the war.

Howitzers were designed to fire their shells upward at an angle (up to 45 degrees) so were able to reach into trenches and the like, which 'line of sight' guns could not. Using a lightweight shell, a range of over 10km was achieved.

Light BG Gun Carrier – 7th March 1918
A badly damaged German 21cm Mörser howitzer being recovered for scrap. The breech has been destroyed – most likely to render it unusable to the enemy, prior to a retreat. Materials were in very short supply as the war dragged on and every attempt was made to salvage and re-process materials as much as possible.

Light BG Gun Carrier – 7th March 1918

There were other ways of moving guns over the 60cm WDLR lines – such as shown here. This system used a pair of bogies to which 'top hat' pattern bolsters were fitted. On either side were stout projecting pegs which engaged with side troughs to carry the load. In use, one bogie would be run clear after the troughs were dropped and the artillery piece manoeuvred into position so as to be drawn up. This view shows the German howitzer from the previous page being loaded. A block and tackle has been secured in front of the leading bogie and a British Westinghouse PE loco is attached to the cabling so as to draw the howitzer up on to the troughs, acting as ramps.

Light BG Gun Carrier – 7th March 1918

The loco is now out of sight, as it draws the howitzer into position.

Light BG Gun Carrier – 7th March 1918
*With the howitzer in position on the troughs, the second bogie is brought
up preparatory to jacking the troughs up to allow it to be positioned.*

A good portrait of the British Westinghouse version of the petrol electric tractors. They differed from the Dick, Kerr in a number of ways – frame cut-outs, lower frame stiffening angle, external leading sandboxes, larger cab side windows (with sliding slotted shutter) and solid engine compartment doors. Note the starting handle left in place. Starting was a problem with both types, the high position of the handle not helping in this respect.

Light BG Gun Carrier – 7th March 1918
The loco is now coupled up to the Gun Carrier and is ready to move away.

CHAPTER FOUR

RESCUING THE WOUNDED

Royal Army Medical Corps: Stretcher Cases & Transport by Rail

THE ROYAL ARMY MEDICAL CORPS were primarily responsible for maintaining the health of the British fighting forces on the Western Front during the 1914-18 War. The nature of this conflict meant that it was essential to treat the wounded with urgency and their retrieval from the battle field was a trial within itself. Quite beside the injuries caused by bullets, shell fragments and the like, the filthy conditions encouraged tetanus and gas gangrene infections, often resulting in complications.

Gathering the injured either during or after a battle, often spread over a broad area, necessitated Collecting Posts, to which men either made their own way (walking wounded) or were carried by a fellow soldier, or by stretcher bearers. Only the most basic medical attention was available at the CPs, and they mainly operated as filters to alleviate congestion further down the system.

The Saving of Soldiers Who Fall in Battle: How the Wounded Man is Removed from the Scene of the Fight to the Dressing Station: The Clearing Hospital: Train to the Base Hospital

Immediately a soldier falls wounded, the medical officer of the man's battalion, whose duties keep him throughout practically within the firing line, attends to him as quickly as he can, and gives first-aid treatment. The wounded man is picked up by his company's stretcher bearers (each infantry company is provided with its stretcher bearers), or by the nearest party from the Bearer Company of the Royal Army

Medical Corps, assisting the battalion bearers. A Bearer Company with its own stretchers is attached to every brigade. In action the stretcher-men keep moving close in rear of the firing line, picking up men as they fall. Each wounded man is taken off to the Dressing Station, as near as convenient in the rear, whence, after further attention, he is removed in one of the Bearer Company's horsed or

motor ambulances in attendance to the Clearing Hospital still further to the rear. There, the case is examined by a senior officer of the RAMC who operates, if necessary. From there the wounded man is removed by train to the Base Hospital, where arrangements are made, according to the gravity of the man's injuries, for shipment home.

The Illustrated War News – October 1914

'Walking' wounded entraining – 7th March 1918
Regular 'D' class wagons being used to transport wounded but walking soldiers to the nearest dressing station. No comfort is provided, only ammunition boxes for sitting on. There are medical orderlies present to tend to the injured and help them on and off the train.

ROYAL ARMY MEDICAL CORPS.

Within a laurel wreath surmounted by a crown the rod of Æsculapius with a serpent entwined. "*In Arduis Fidelis.*"

HISTORY AND TRADITIONS.

It was not until the Peninsular War that medical officers were appointed to accompany an army in the field. During the long reign of peace which followed Waterloo, ordinary cases of sickness were looked after by regimental surgeons and hospital sergeants in regimental hospitals, so that when war against Russia came suddenly upon England in 1854, the medical organisation was found sadly wanting. The Army Hospital Corps was then organised the first school being formed at Chatham. Since then the changes in medical organisation have been many, the present title of Royal Army Medical Corps dating from 1898. From the earliest days the medical service has a history second to none in personal devotion to that army of which it is an essential part. No real reform in the soldier's condition but may be traced to the urgent representation of the medical officer, who, in the hard days of past neglect and want of sympathy with the soldier, never faltered in devotion to his betterment, and triumphed in the end. The record of the medical branch of the British Army is indeed a glorious one, those cases alone which have been officially recognised having gained more Victoria Crosses than any other individual corps in the British Army.

Left: Contemporary postcard celebrating the RAMC, both the dress uniform and field uniform is shown. Below: Stretcher cases on a forward area tramway being pushed from an Advanced Dressing Station to a point where there could be collected by an ambulance – or moved by train to a Casualty Clearing Station.

So as to make the passage of the injured back behind the lines as quick as possible, for those who could be treated, a system of 'triage' was introduced. Soldiers were divided into three groups; first – those with light injuries who could be treated quickly and returned to duty, second – those who needed hospitalisation and third – those so badly injured that resources might not be able to save. These latter received little in the way of attention, other than being kept as comfortable as circumstances allowed.

The first line of treatment was in the field, as close to the front as possible, at an Advanced Dressing Station, often situated in a communication trench. Here, under an officer of the RAMC would be a Sergeant, Corporal and two or more 'other ranks' to deal with incomers. Also, there were stretcher-bearers (often drawn from the Regimental Band)

and sufficient supplies of basic medical supplies, such as bandages, gauze, anti-tetanus, ointments etc, to treat the injured as well as possible before they were passed back down the line. The Medical Officer would oversee this and, as there was no holding capacity, performed the difficult task of deciding the order of who went on to the next stage.

From the ADS, the injured were passed back to a Casualty Clearing Station (see diagram page 42). These were the first position where actual surgery took place and the closest to the front that nursing staff were allowed. There would be upwards of 50 beds and 150 stretchers, enabling around 200 men to be handled at any given time. The staff ran to seven RAMC Medical Officers including a dentist, plus many orderlies and a Quartermaster. When casualties exceeded capacity, and it was not possible to pass men back

to the hospitals in the rear, emergency surgical teams came forwards to deal with urgent cases. Accommodation would be wooden huts (often the portable type) or under canvas.

From the CCS those requiring further, or more specialised treatment were passed back to one of the Hospitals established well behind the front line, each with a capacity of at least 400 men. Often this was by standard gauge ambulance train but use of the canal systems meant specially adapted barges were also used. Each Division had two 'Stationary Hospitals' capable of taking 400 men and in addition there would be a larger 'General Hospital' – often established in commandeered large hotels or similar big buildings. These were also used as Convalescent Depots. Many men though would be returned to home soil – a 'Blighty one'.

Possibly the train seen on page 105 – here shown loading men on to a waiting lorry, north of Poperinghe Road. The tractor is a Dick, Kerr petrol electric – with two intriguing angle shields fitted above the radiator. Note many of the 5th Army soldiers with 'Brodie' steel helmets have fabric covers fitted. The covers eliminated any possible chance of light reflection from the helmet, which could otherwise attract the unwelcome attention of an enemy sniper.

USE OF THE LIGHT RAILWAYS

To get to the CCS from the ADS, the light railways proved very useful, as horse drawn and motor ambulances often struggled in the adverse conditions of churned up muddy terrain. Push trolleys, more commonly used to convey munitions to the front, were used to move the wounded, though their journey must have been very uncomfortable due to the lack of springing.

Once the loco worked part of the system was reached, they could be transferred to larger wagons, usually 'D' class, where the 'walking' wounded would be packed in,

sitting and standing as they were able. Stretcher cases were often laid on transverse timber supports, as below, open to the elements apart from a blanket. RAMC orderlies would accompany the casualties on their way to the CCS.

By 1918 an adapted 'D' class was available that allowed the stretchers to be stacked and provided some protection at least. There were also purpose built 'Ambulance Vans' (see page 214). They were bulky and tall vehicles and no more comfortable than any of the others.

In addition to the RAMC, the British Red Cross Society provided staff and equipment for the rescue and treatment of the wounded. See the contemporary cigarette card, most likely from a packet of 'Woodbines', reproduced on the right.

Below: A 20hp Simplex tractor hauling 'D' class and 'E' class bogie wagons loaded with stretcher cases, passing a 12 inch gun on railway mounting. Timber cross members support the upper tier – but men were laid on stretchers in the wagon beds as well. Note that the Simplex has unusual 'tramcar' pressed spoked wheels. Outskirts of Arras.

Ambulance Wagon – 7th March 1918

An adapted 'D' wagon to carry twelve stretcher cases – supported on racks set in the bed of the wagon. One stretcher was usually left free, as storage space for kit, etc. They were protected (from the weather at least) by roll down canvas side sheets, bearing a red cross on a white circle. A kit of conversion parts, for both 'D' and 'E' class wagons was available. Beside the stretchers and racks a simple framed roof, covered by a tarpaulin, was supported by wooden ends, both of which had a curiously inaccessible lidded box. The 'E' class conversion was less common, as these wagons only had a single central door on each side, making loading and unloading the stretcher cases more difficult.

CHAPTER FIVE
MAINTAINING THE SYSTEM
Central Light Railway Workshops: Vox Vrie Yard: Workshop Train: 60cm Cranes

PRIOR TO THE AUTUMN OF 1916 the repair of Decauville locos, trucks and wagons was carried out in one corner of Audruicq Yard. A Directorate of Light Railways being formed with General Twining as DLR and Colonel O'Brien as DDLR. A plan was put forward and approved on 20 November 1916 for building the Light Railway repair shops in the neighbourhood of Béthune and an order for buildings and machine tools for these shops was placed on 4 January 1917. For several reasons, the main one being that Béthune was perhaps too near the front line, the site of the Workshops was changed from Béthune to La Laque adjoining Berguette station on 12 December 1916 and the site was finally approved by the French on 31 December 1916.

The La Laque site was very suitable on account of its proximity to the Aire canal for water for the Power House and its railway facilities, adjoining as it did, the Berguette-Hazebrouk and Berguette-Aire main line. Also the site provided ample room for the necessary CSCP (Central Salvage Collection Park) storage ground.

Major John Bowden was appointed DADLR in charge of the layout, erection equipment and maintenance of the works. This office commenced duties at Le Laque on 26 January 1917. The work, in the first place, was undertaken by the 17th battalion Northumberland Fusiliers Trades Company – strengthened by the 23rd Light Railway Miscellaneous Trades Company on 15 March and the 26th Light Railway Workshop Company on 23 March – assisted later by a Company of Prisoners of War (POW).

The first barges arrived with material on 18 January, and the first pile driven for the Broad Gauge Traffic Bridge over the Aire canal on the 17th. Hard frost commenced on the 21st and delayed foundation work until 12 February. The first consignment of machinery arrived on 26 February and the first building completed (Administrative Office) on 15 March, 115 days after approval of the scheme. Work proceeded steadily until interrupted by a blizzard, which stopped all work on the site for a few days following 18 March, four Erecting Shop trusses being blown down.

The object of the Workshops was mainly for the repair of locos, tractors and wagons in use by the Light Railways in the five Armies and Lines of Communication, although a variety of miscellaneous work for the Armies in France was undertaken. In addition, a large stores of spare parts for vehicles was necessary, and a regular distribution of these stores to the various Armies commenced on 19 April 1917.

One drawback of the site was the swampy nature of the low lying ground but this was overcome by filling in a great portion of the site with black and red mine earth from the adjacent colliery at Estrée Blanche. To a great extent this was carried out by Chinese labour, the first detachment arriving 1 May. Much assistance was obtained by use of the 24th and 34th POW Companies but, owing to the decision that these POW had to be employed a certain distance from the front line, they were withdrawn on 22 May, causing considerable disorganisation of the unskilled work.

The following dates are of interest:

16-05-17	Smith's Shop open
23-05-17	First machine ran in the Machine Shop
28-05-17	First overhead electrical 10 ton travelling crane in Erecting Shop used
2-06-17	First casting made in Foundry
04-06-17	First ROD broad gauge took water from permanent water supply in Yard
17-06-17	Work started on repairs to first loco, Cooke 'American' type No 900 in Erecting Shop
17-07-17	Double shift commenced in all Shops

The personnel of the Shops comprised:
23rd Light Railways Miscellaneous Trades Company
25th Light Railway Workshop Company
26th Light Railway Workshop Company
27th Light Railway Workshop Company
24th Light Railways Miscellaneous Trades Company

Beaurainville, repairs to Broad Gauge Caledon Lorries.[1] For this purpose a new building 300ft x 30ft x 27ft high, with new overhead cranes was ordered from England and erected on the new site. Upon the alteration of this arrangement, when it was decided that maintenance of the Caledon lorries should be undertaken by the Senior Tractor Officer, the Caledon Lorry Shop was converted for repairs to Steam Road Rollers, Broad Gauge Cranes etc.

A new extension (100ft) of the Erecting Shop and overhead crane gantry had been, previous to the evacuation, ordered from England, and this arrived overseas in time for the combined erection with the old buildings. This portion, the Caledon Lorry Shop, Foundry and Garage buildings constitute the only 'new' Works buildings at Beaurainville. The Foundry and Garage were constructed from standard building sections, the fabrication of which, eventually, developed as output of these workshops.

The system operating for the water supply at Beaurainville is as follows:

Two Rees Roturbo motor driven pumps, each with a capacity of 7,500 gallons per hour pump from a spring situated in the grounds of a Chateau at Beaurainville and deliver water to a 35,000 gallon tank with a 130ft head. This tank feeds the Works, Camp, the adjoining ROD Camp, Broad Gauge Engines and three POW Camps. The fire mains are served from a 50,000 gallon tank with a 125ft head. Water is pumped into this tank from the river Canche – which separates the Works from the Camp at Beaurainville, by steam pumps located in the Power House.

The following are dates of interest concerning the re commencement of these Works:

1) Formerly Scottish Commercial Cars. Caledon Industrial Motor Vehicles, Duke Street works, Glasgow, launched the Caledon in 1915. It was a bonneted chain-driven four-wheel lorry with a Dorman engine (similar to the engines in Simplex tractors).

30-04-18	Arrival of first train of material at Beaurainville.
20-05-18	Power supplied by temporary set.
23-05-18	First Decauville train run.
24-05-18	Camp site – work commenced.
25-05-18	Excavation for Power House commenced.
29-05-18	Concreting commenced (Works).
01-06-18	Administration Office erected.
04-06.18	POW labour commenced.
10-06-18	First stanchion of Shops erected.
14-06-18	Main Shop roof sheeting commenced.
27-06-18	Pile driving for bridge connecting Works with Camp commenced.
28-06-18	Road Roller Shed erected.
03-07-18	Sheeting of Constructional Shop commenced.
19-07-18	First wagon completed repair at Beaurainville.
02-08-18	First loco completed repairs at Beaurainville.
12-08-18	Change of Directorate – Central LR Works renamed CME (LR) Works and transferred from DLR's control to CME.
17-08-18	Power House commenced running.

Short history of the Central Light Railway Workshops
9 May 1919

From November 1918, after the Armistice was signed, the WDLR continued operating well into 1919. During this period they were used to evacuate troops and equipment from the field while also supplying those remaining with food and other essential items. Humanely, this service was extended to the struggling local population. Beaurainville remained busy during this period, repairing locos, tractors and wagons. The precise date of the Works closure has not been recorded – though late 1919/20 is likely.

Beaurainville

Page opposite: The wagons all had chilled cast iron wheels, (the chill providing a hard wearing surface between wheel and rail) these were produced by the major manufacturer of railway wheel sets, Hadfields of Sheffield. Eventually these wheels would wear hollow and require replacement.

The locomotives had cast iron wheel centres and a steel tyre. When these wore they could be re-profiled, the process being undertaken using one of the two wheel lathes seen set below floor level in the back of the photo. This made the handling of the wheels easier as they did not require lifting as far with the overhead travelling crane which spans this bay of the shop. The process of re-profiling the tyres of a locomotive could be carried out several times until it was deemed that the tyre had become too thin for further safe use. At this point the old tyre would be either pulled or cut off the wheel centre and a new tyre fitted. New steel tyres were supplied by companies such as Steel, Peech & Tozer of Rotherham, who forged and pierced the tyre blank before rolling it to the required diameter and flange profile. The inside would be left under size so that it could be bored to suit the size of the wheel centre. The man in the right foreground is operating a vertical boring machine, probably a Webster Bennett, and is engaged in machining the centre of a new tyre. This will be done precisely (approximately one thousandth of an inch smaller in diameter than the outside diameter of the wheel) so as to allow a shrink fit on the wheel centre. After being machined to size, the tyre would be set horizontally on a firebrick hearth so that the outside could be evenly heated by a ring of gas jets. Once judged hot enough, the wheel centre and, probably, the other wheel and axle supported vertically by a crane above, would be lowered into the middle of the tyre, which would then cool and contract onto the wheel centre. A large sledge hammer or two would be kept near just in case the wheel did not go squarely into the tyre.

Typical of the period is the drive to the machinery by flat belting. Each machine had a device enabling the belt to be engaged, or run loose. It is also interesting to note the lack of guarding to the flapping flat belt drive and the absence of any personal protective equipment, such as overalls and safety glasses etc, all deemed so important today. Again, some of the workers are German POWs.

Collection: Paul Ingham

Beaurainville
Standard Gauge 'Mobile Power Station No.3'
on duty at the Light Railway Workshops.
              Collection: Bob Barlow

Beaurainville
Stored locomotives – see page opposite.

Beaurainville

60cm locomotives in storage, this view looking North-West from the right hand side of the site. From left to right: line one – Alco 2-6-2T, line two – Barclay and Hudson-Hudswell 0-6-0WT (one with a steel cab back sheet) plus some captured German Feldbahn 0-8-0T, line three – Hunslet 4-6-0T, then three lines of Baldwin 4-6-0T locos. Note the first loco in line two is one of the 'A' class 0-4-0WT Hudson-Hudswell locos supplied in 1916 to 2ft 6ins gauge but converted later to 60cm.

In the background on the left can be seen the main building, steaming shed just off centre and one of the water tanks centre right.

Ramp for off-loading locomotive from normal gauge tracks – 7th March 1918

After repair at Berguette and later, Beaurainville, the locomotives were shipped back to where they were needed on standard gauge flat wagons. On arrival, the wagon would be backed up to a prepared slope formed of cribbed timber – sleepers being favourite. This was a difficult task, fraught with problems plus a degree of risk.

Untitled

Off-loading repaired tractors was much simpler. In this image, a Dick, Kerr 4w PE is being lowered down after being lifted from the standard gauge flat wagon on which it was delivered. The steel frame and chain tackle was a standard item and another set can be seen on page 126. Note the way that the 60cm track crosses the standard gauge, lower right.

Note the increased ventilation in the radiator shield as compared to that shown on page 176. Also the re-railing bar.

VOX VRIE YARD

Named after a nearby farm, Vox Vrie Yard, seen in the above panorama (three photographs), was situated between Woeste and Poperinghe (Flanders). It was well equipped for running repairs in the field and also reclamation of components from rolling stock too damaged to repair at all. From left to right can be seen:

Water Supply
Stores
Carpenters & Smith's Shops
Workshop Train
Engine Lift
Portable Shed (under construction)
Six ton Crane
Locomotive, Tractor and Wagon Repair Sidings

The two water supply pipes and taps around the site would have been fed from a large tank or tanks, located on the site (though not revealed in the photographs), itself fed by pump from a water source nearby.

A WDLR pattern timber 'portable' locomotive shed was under construction so, possibly, the yard was being expanded at the time of the cameraman's visit. Both steam and tractor lifts/hoists were already in use and behind the shed, a Ransomes & Rapier 6 ton crane was deployed for lifting tractors and wagons also. These cranes were restricted to yard areas, as their weight and bulk made them less than suitable for work where the track was poor.

Although largely unseen in the panorama, one of the Workshop Trains (see pages 201-213) is in use behind the shed. Study of the photographs on subsequent pages show that rudimentary camouflage had been applied to the roofs – in the form of netting and branches etc. It is unlikely this was required at Vox Vrie, so is likely to have been applied when the train was at an earlier location nearer the front line. In addition to the six vehicles that composed the train, there was a seventh, a sawmill fitted to an 'F' class bogie wagon. A simple overall roof was supported by timbers located in the side pockets – which usually accepted vertical stanchions. Canvas drop down side sheets were provided for protection against wind and rain.

The sawbench was electrically driven, via a belt from large motor mounted on the timbered deck. This latter also covered the centre well, which was unused, apart from collecting sawdust. This set-up would permit, amongst other things, the rapid manufacture of replacement timbers for wagon repair and many other purposes.

An area (on the right) was reserved for breaking up wagons, some parts, like wheels and bogies being recovered for refurbishment and those no longer capable of re-use being sent back to one of the salvage yards (see photo pages 72-73). Given the equipment available, all but the most damaged wagons would be recoverable at Vox Vrie.

Most running repairs on steam locomotives and tractors would be possible, the Workshop Train providing the machining capabilities required to make all manner of parts. This was of value, as locos and tractors could be kept in service longer, without recourse to a time consuming return to the main repair shops.

Extreme left is a water column, for filling locomotives, (a similar column can be seen in the distance on the third photograph). Stood on trestles, outside the Stores building is the distorted chassis of an 'E' class wagon, devoid of all upper work and timbers. Note the horseshoe placed on the drums near the open doorway. Leaning up against the building on the right (Carpenters Shop) are two newly prepared notice boards, bearing the legend 'Officers Quarters, No Thoroughfare'.

Vox Vrie Yard – 7th March 1918

In the left background is the Smith's Shop and, next to it, a portable sawmill on an 'F' type wagon chassis (see page 133). Going right, behind the engine lift, can be glimpsed one of the Workshop Trains ordered for the WDLR. In front stands a line of locomotives, two Simplex 40hp 'Open' tractors, two PE tractors (one Westinghouse and one Dick, Kerr) and a line of Baldwin and Alco steam locomotives. Centre foreground is a line of wagons, all 'D' class awaiting attention. Note the timber 'stop' on the siding on which they are standing. It comprises two transverse timbers, braced by a cruciform planted into the ground and reinforced by a pile of aggregate. Note the loco coal pile in front of the sawmill.

Vox Vrie Yard – 7th March 1918

The frame of a badly damaged 'D' class wagon stands in the foreground, with bogie frames, wheelsets and sundry parts to the right and behind. More wagons await on the sidings. In the fields beyond the yard, three haystacks stand in the distance.

Untitled

*Vox Vrie Yard – the engine lift with a Baldwin 4-6-*OT*. Workshop Train on the right.*

2.06.8

Untitled

Vox Vrie Yard, a Ransomes & Rapier six ton crane (see page 139) lifting a 40hp 'open' Simplex tractor. Portable loco shed under construction in the background. The bogies of the wagon body can be seen on the track behind it.

Repair Train at work – 7th March, 1918
Vox Vrie Yard

Above, Two photo spread of the Workshop Train at Vox Vrie, seen from the operating side. Pages 131 and 132 carry larger images of each.

Right: Two views of a Workshop Train in operation at other locations.

Repair Train at work – 7th March, 1918
*Vox Vrie Yard – Machinery wagons 1 & 2 (centre & right), with roof camouflage. At the left
is the Tool van and Stores Van. The larger soldier carrying the gauge, is the WO2 (Mechanist
Sergeant Major) – in charge of all tradesman in the workshop. He is holding a 'master'
calibrating gauge, probably for loco pressure gauges.*

Repair Train at work – 7th March, 1918

Vox Vrie Yard – the generator car contained two 10KW Aster petrol generating sets, flanking a
centrally mounted air compressor by Messrs Reavell of Ipswich, itself driven by a 10HP electric
motor. Note the jumper cables carrying current between the vehicles – and the
shaded electric light over the right hand petrol engine.

Workshop Train 'Saw' – 7th March, 1918
Vox Vrie Yard

This improvised portable sawmill was a useful addition to the workshop train parked nearby. The decking has been replaced with heavier planks to support the weight of the heavy saw with its cast iron frame and large electric motor. Note the unguarded blade and ubiquitous cigarette in the sawyer's mouth – dangerous in such a flammable and dusty environment. Note the lower planks of the drop well have been removed to allow removal of the sawdust falling between the floor planks.

Untitled

Work on the track at a marshalling yard being undertaken. Heavy use demanded constant maintenance, which required skilled labour – often experienced men drawn from UK railway companies. A Dick, Kerr 4W PE stands with a train of materials. Due to the cramped cab on these locomotives, the crew have hung their respirator cases and helmets on the outside. Notice that the permanent way gang fettling the sidings do not have steel helmets or respirators – so this location is out of range of direct shell fire.

Untitled

*The track and ballasting is neat and shows no sign of the random and often violent
disturbances that yards closer to the front were subject to.*

Untitled

A 20hp Simplex petrol tractor under repair, with another seen dimly behind. Note
the two men on the right, repairing a radiator. One is using a small hearth with hand
operated blower to heat the irons while the other is making a solder repair. The use of
existing buildings was common, (see page 52 for probable location).

Untitled

However rudimentary, the arrangement of this 'Portable Shed' has been well thought out with a shallow pit enabling easy access to the motion for examination and servicing. Being covered, repairs could be undertaken in most weathers. Also the design was open at the top, allowing smoke and steam to escape. The two men in front of the open smokebox door are most likely cleaning the tubes whilst others are inspecting the motion and repairing or taking up glands. The man on top is attending to a leaking whistle valve. Behind, another Baldwin waits for attention.

Note the shed cladding boards (right) have been used as a makeshift blackboard to explain or check the valve settings of some forgotten locomotive – plus proof that even in wartime, humour shines through!

Untitled

Wagon repair siding at 'Q' dump Arras. Compare the sheds in the background to those shown on page 53. A 'D' class timber framed bogie is being worked on. It is supported under the shear-legs by a purpose made spreader bar.

On the extreme right is a 'B' class 4w open wagon and, next in line, an intriguing vehicle looking very much like a coach – details for which nothing can be traced. It is difficult to tell, due to the foreshortening, if it is a bogie vehicle or 4w.

Untitled

Hunslet No.370 being righted after derailing. The cranes were worked by hand, with side mounted platforms so that two men could operate each of the long crank handles. Hand operated cranes were notoriously dangerous as, should the ratchet pawl fail or become disengaged, the men on the handles suddenly bore the entire weight being lifted.

The cranes were built by Ransome & Rapier Ltd of Ipswich. They would lift, when propped in place, 6 tons at a radius of 18 feet (double rope) or 11 tons at 24 feet (single rope). They proved too heavy for use on poorly laid trackwork – which greatly restricted their usefulness. The French had smaller, more versatile 60cm cranes made under the 'Magnard System'. Some were made in the UK by Chambers & Scott & Co. Ltd of Motherwell.

Untitled

The locomotive is righted and now held by chain slings directly under the front and rear beams. Given the number of men and officers present, it is likely that the photos represent an exercise for the cameraman. While getting a crane either end of the stricken loco would be easy in a yard with passing tracks, there was no such opportunity en-route.

Untitled

Hunslet No.370 ready to lower back onto the track. Note the R&R cranes were supported on no less than four 4w bogies each with a very small wheelbase. Provision was made for increasing lateral stability by passing sections of steel joist between the bogie pairs at either end. A feature not commonly found on small cranes was the ability to crank the whole crane upperworks backwards or forwards, the side members being supported by pairs of rollers.

Untitled

*As the locomotive was lowered onto the rails, brute force from
the crew became necessary for the final alignment. Swinging
the loco into position as the flanges came down on to the
railhead demanded skill, care and strength. Hunslet No.370
was from the third batch – note the re-railing ramp carried
vertically over the front tank stay.*

Line cut by shell fire – 7th March 1918

The closer tracks were to the front, the more likely they were to be disrupted by enemy action. Here a 40HP 'open' Simplex petrol tractor is drawn up to a shell damaged section of track. In the background can be seen another railway embankment. Steel sleepered track was readily replaced, however, and trains would soon be moving again …

CHAPTER SIX
LOCOMOTIVES & TRACTORS
Steam Locomotives: Internal Combustion: Petrol Electrics: Crewe Tractor

NCE THE DEFICIENCIES of front line transport had been highlighted during the winter of 1915-16 and the usefulness of 'home made' tramways was noted, the British War Office took steps to remedy the situation. Essential for the proposed lines was motive power, steam being the first consideration. Initially, on expert advice, from the likes of E R Calthrop, a gauge of 2ft 6ins was considered, but common sense prevailed and 60cm was adopted, providing ready compatibility with both the French and German (if captured) lines and equipment.

STEAM LOCOMOTIVES

Small numbers of locomotives and associated narrow gauge equipment, including track had been ordered prior to 1916 however. Robert Hudson of Leeds provided 0-4-0WT steam locomotives (see above)[1], plus there was an experimental 0-4-0 internal combustion tractor design from McEwan-

Pratt (see page 168). The foregoing were mainly intended for use on construction work (camps, quarries and the like) – generally conducted in areas well behind the lines. They were not used to convey ammunition or supplies.

From the outbreak of the War, most of UK locomotive builders became increasingly involved with the production of armaments etc., such that, by the time the need for light railway motive power was required in 1916, order books were full and little capacity remained.

HUDSON
HUDSWELL 0-6-0WT

Given that Robert Hudson was the largest supplier of light railway material in Britain at the time, it is probably

natural they were approached with regards not just to locomotives but to track and rolling stock also. Hudson did not, though, actually make locos themselves and contracted this work out – though Robert Hudson plates were fitted. In the case of the War Department enquiry an 0-6-0WT design was suggested, based on the class 'G' loco made by Hudswell Clarke. The first four left Hudswell's Jack Lane Works (Leeds) in May-June 1916 – despite having been ordered in October 1914. The cost of each locomotive was £460.00 and further small orders were made subsequently. Encouraged

Photos: collection Roy C Link

---

1 – Some were built to 2ft 6in gauge, later being re-gauged by the Army to 60cm. One can be seen in storage at Beaurainville on page 121.

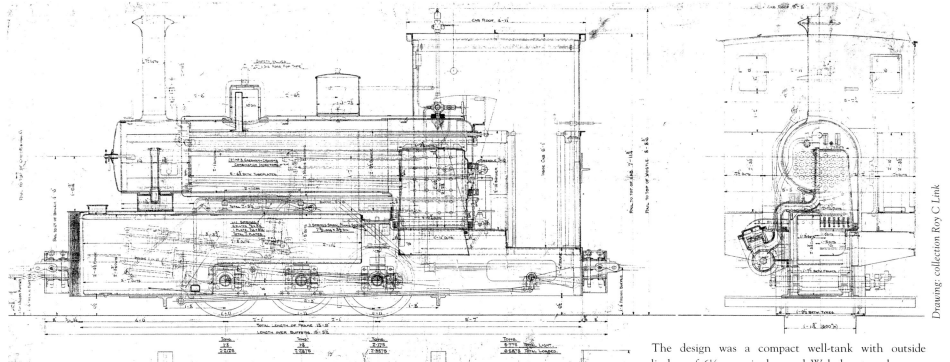

Drawing: collection Roy C Link

The design was a compact well-tank with outside cylinders of 6½ x 12 inches and Walschaerts valve gear capable of running on lightweight 20LB rail round curves of 65ft radius. Driving wheels were 23ins in diameter on a wheelbase of 50ins; the centre wheel was flangeless. Single cast iron brake blocks acted on the leading axle. The leading and centre axleboxes were sprung by inverted springs mounted on top of the frames while the rear axle boxes had a separate transverse spring fixed between the frames, just behind the internal water tank.

A copper firebox and brass tubes were provided with a boiler (working pressure 180psi) made of "best steel plates, well lagged and neatly finished with iron casing". The nominal horsepower was 30hp and the tractive force 2909LBS.

On level track it was claimed a load of 150 tons could

by the useful deployment of light railway equipment on the Somme in 1916 (see photograph on page x), an order for thirty more similar machines was placed with Robert Hudson in August of that year.

be hauled, this dropping to a mere 26 tons on a gradient of 1 in 30. Speed was stated to be between 7 to 8 miles per hour. The cab was open above the waist, apart from a front spectacle sheet and this gave rise to 'in the field' modifications in attempts to protect the crew from the worst of the weather, not to mention small arms fire and shrapnel. Being well tanks the centre of gravity was low and the weight relatively well distributed. This made them good performers on the less than well laid-tracks over which they often ran.

They were sufficiently robust that a number survived the conflict to pass into civilian hands after the Armistice. The design continued to be offered in Robert Hudson's post-war catalogues up to the 1930s. By this time inflation had pushed the price up to £2040.00.

ANDREW BARCLAY 0-6-0WT

These locomotives are very elusive and only rarely appear in photographs. The specification required was as the Hudson Hudswell 0-6-0WT locos, but placed with Andrew Barclay Limited of Kilmarnock when Hudson's sub-contractor could not meet demand due to pressure of work in progress.

Delivery was early in 1917 and a total of 25 locos were built in one batch. Their WDLR numbers were 601-625. All were delivered to Flanders where they came under the Australian Railway Corps. W J K Davies (*Light Railways of the First World War*) noted – '...who liked them so much they refused to part with them, and took them with them when they moved'.

Although these locomotives followed the general design of the Hudsons, there were noticeable differences. Most obvious was the Belpaire firebox, less so, the slightly larger 26ins dia driving wheels and 52ins wheelbase. The length over frames though, was nearly 8ins shorter. A pair of springs were provided either side for the axleboxes and the brake blocks only acted on the leading axle. These were operated by a weighted lever as opposed to the more usual

Barclay Catalogue image – collection Roy C Link

screw handbrake. Another novelty was the outside regulator valve and live steam pipes. In service these required lagging to avoid heat loss. Both of these features were more common on small European locos, such as those built by Orenstein & Koppel, whose products Barclay emulated. If anything, the cab left the crew even less protected than the Hudson locos, the front spectacle being very meagre.

COUPLINGS

Neither the Hudson nor Barclay designs used the 'standard' WDLR coupler casting – which required its sprung drawbar to extend behind the headstock of whatever it was applied to. As both these locos had well tanks this was not feasible, so they had alternative arrangements. On the Hudson a cast coupler pocket, with a vertical pin, was bolted on the

frame end and was provided a curved buffing face, made from flat plate. The Barclay locos had a better arrangement with a curved, vertically-slotted casting, which held a bar ending in a WDLR 'spectacle' link.

HUNSLET ENGINE COMPANY 4-6-0T

Something far more complex was required for the purposes of a proper light railway system and the Hunslet Engine Company, Leeds, was approached with regard suitable motive power. They provided a re-design of their 'HANS SAUER' 0-6-0T design, modified to the 4-6-0 wheel arrangement and well within the 4 ton axle load (at 3 tons 10 cwt) limit specified. The new design could haul 286 tons on the level and traverse curves down to 100ft radius. An initial order for ten was placed The first built, Hunslet

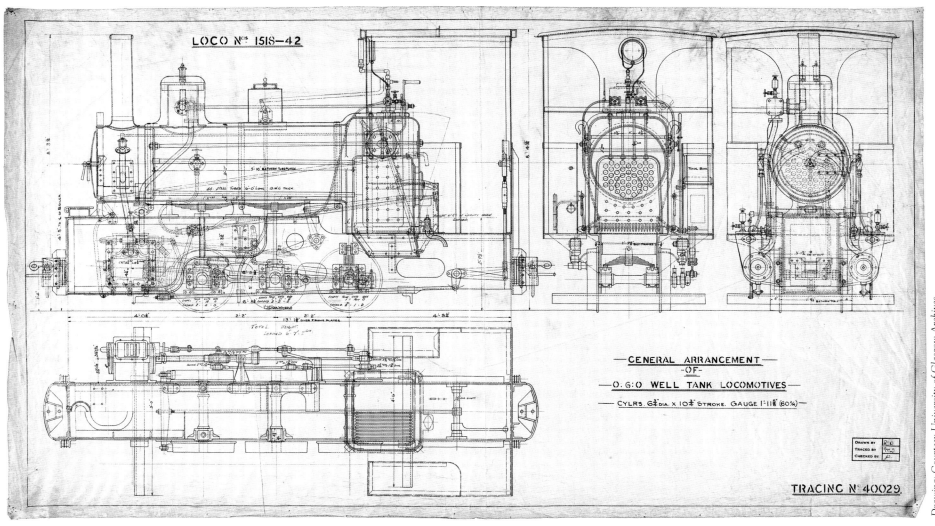

LOCO Nᵒˢ 1518—42

GENERAL ARRANGEMENT
-OF-
O.6.O WELL TANK LOCOMOTIVES
— CYLRS. 6¾"DIA. x 10¾" STROKE. GAUGE 1'-11⅝" (60%) —

TRACING Nᵒ 40029.

Drawing: Courtesy University of Glasgow Archives

Above: The Andrew Barclay general arrangement drawing for the WDLR 0-6-0WT tank locomotives the company built to a similar specification as those made by Hudson-Hudswell. Whereas the water tank in the latter occupied a space between the frames nearly as far back as the rear axle, the Barclay seems to have had less water space,

extending back to just in front of the centre axle. The tank was a little wider though, being part of the frames and not a dropped-in unit.

The Belpaire firebox had its foundation ring above the frames allowing a wide grate and the frames below had cut-outs either side for access to the ashpan for cleaning.

Typical of Barclay products of the period was the external regulator valve mounted on the side of the steam dome. As a result, the regulator handle in the cab was off centre and higher up than usual. Also a weighted lever worked the brake, which operated shoes on the leading axle only.

Hunslet Works No.1216 (WDLR No.304), one of the first batch of ten locomotives, built under War Office Order No.DRT 648. The Hunslet order book records "engines to be painted dull black". Seen here in photographic grey livery.

Works No.1213 (WDLR No.301), was ready for inspection by MOD agents, Rendell, Palmer & Triton in June. By early August 1916 the first loco arrived in France.

With the benefit of hindsight the choice of wheel arrangement must be questioned – as might the use of inside frames, especially when most of Hunslet's 2ft gauge locomotives had outside frames. Certainly the Americans required all their Great War steam locos to be built as 2-6-2T's, a far better arrangement for easy running in both directions. The later ALCO built locos ordered by the WDLR had the 2-6-2 arrangement and outside frames.

Five batches were built by Hunslet during the period 1916-19, totalling 155 locomotives. The last few, completed after the Armistice and now surplus, being gauged for 2ft 6ins in the hope of finding sales overseas. Relatively few modifications were made during the construction period. Most notable was Hunslet Works No.1287 (WDLR No.375) which was made with steam condensing gear. This was an attempt to create a steam locomotive less obvious to the enemy when working close to the front. While judged a success, the increased availability (and reliability) of the

Left: WDLR No.304 again, this time posed on curved track – demonstrating the promised 100ft radius which the locomotives would "traverse with ease". Note the coupler swing and traversing jack – two of these were actually supplied with each loco, as were a pair of loco lamps.

Right: A rear view as above.

Photos: courtesy Hunslet Archives

larger Simplex tractors meant this was not pursued. After trials, the condensing gear was removed. Oil firing was also experimented with.

They were popular locomotives with crews, being more stable on the poor track than the wider Baldwin locos. The side tanks also gave a somewhat lower centre of gravity. Most light railway units that had Hunslets tried as hard as they could to keep them. Also, unlike all the other WDLR steam locomotives, they had a fully enclosed cab.

Like the Barclay locos mentioned earlier, the Hunslet design also had a Belpaire pattern firebox. This slotted between the frames over the centre pair of coupled wheels resulting in a very narrow grate and ashpan. To combat the lack of width the firebox was quite long, at 4ft 6ins overall, this provided an internal grate area of just under

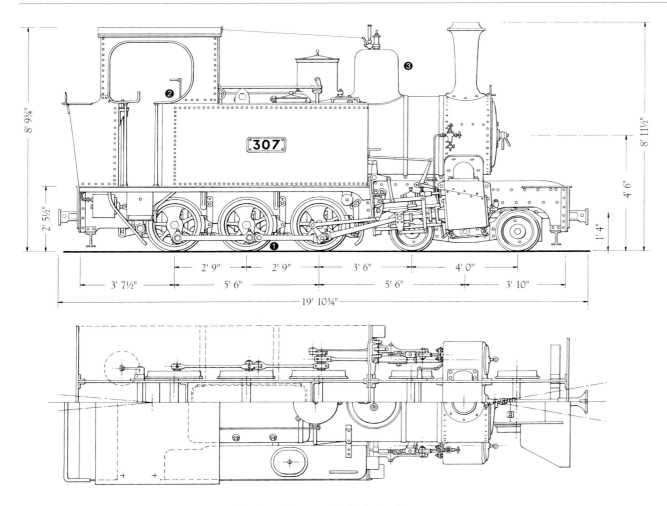

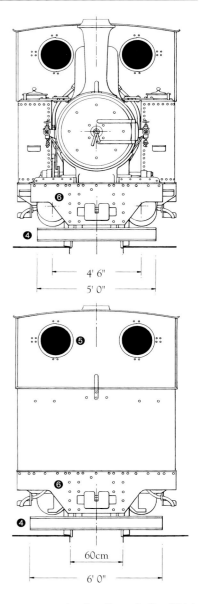

Hunslet built 4-6-0T – as originally built. Driving wheels 2ft 0in dia. Bogie wheels 1ft 6½in dia.

❶ – *Flanged centre driving wheels on locos WDLR Nos.301– 345. Flangeless from No.346 onward.*
❷ – *Water lifters and piping to tanks on locos from No.346.* ❸ – *Steam delivery valve added to front of dome from No.346.* ❹ – *Front and rear derailment beams made from rolled steel joists replaced by flat bottom rail from 346 onward.* ❺ – *Rear cab windows originally unprotected. Horizontal bars on locos from No.346.* ❻ – *Coil spring coupler centralising gear added to both buffer beams from WDLR No.2323 (November 22nd 1917).*

WDLR HUNSLET
4-6-0T

12in.   0   1   2   3   4   5 Feet

Scale: 1:43·5 – 7mm equals 1 foot. Drawn by Roy C Link

The Hunslet 4-6-0t was a handsome locomotive, as
exemplified in this front left hand three-quarter view.
Unusually, for the period, there was no footplating
forward of the side tanks – but this did afford much
better access to the cylinders and motion.

Photo: courtesy Hunslet Archives

Page opposite: Hunslet General Arrangement drawing for the later batches of WDLR 4-6-0T showing the various modifications made to the original design. These include: Water lifting injector, flangeless centre driving wheels, auxiliary steam valve on dome, derailment bars made from lengths of rail. Note from the notes upper right that the working pressure was increased from 160LBS per sq inch to 180LBS.

Right: Hunslet Works No.1287, which was modified with condensing apparatus so as to consume its steam and smoke.

The experimental condensing apparatus, when in use, heated the water in the tanks to such a level that the backhead injectors would no longer function. To combat this, a steam feedwater pump was provided – fixed behind the cab steps. This fed to a clack valve on the boiler. Note also the mud door on the base of the boiler – added with the water lifter. This allowed the removal of detritus carried in with dirty water from shell holes.

Photo: courtesy Hunslet Archives

four square feet. Boiler pressure was 160LBS and there has never been any suggestion that the type ever struggled for steam. Outside Walschaerts motion meant servicing was straightforward, most of the oiling undertaken when preparing the locos not requiring access between the frames, which were only just over 1ft 6ins apart.

The driving axles had conventional leaf springs augmented by rubber blocks in an attempt to protect the springs against rough track. There was no compensation between the driving wheels and front truck. Couplers, to

the standard WDLR pattern (based on the French 60cm design) were firmly anchored to the chassis on long shanks, which were sprung at the inner end.

As successive batches were manufactured, some modifications were made and one noticeable alteration was the replacement of the front and rear sections of steel joist, set some 3ins above the railhead, with sections of rail instead. Also, while the first locomotives had flanges on all driving wheels, they were removed from the centre axle in later batches – something that also happened with

the Baldwin locos. By 1917 a forward-facing auxiliary steam valve was added to the front of the steam dome. In addition, a water lifting injector was fitted, supply being into the left hand side-tank, along with hose brackets on the back of the bunker (see page 95).

After the war, Hunslet built a further nine locomotives to this design, all for 2ft gauge apart from one built to 2ft 6ins. There were though, any number of surplus locos available and a number of these were returned to Hunslet for gauge conversion or other modifications.

Untitled

A working party of British troops going up to the forward area, Elveringhe, near Ypres, February 1917. Hunslet 4-6-0T No.309, still carrying the supplied loco lamp on the front iron, lettered for the 'Railway Operating Department' with a train of French Decauville 'DV' all-steel bogie open wagons. These had been acquired in March 1916 when the British took over French lines around Hersin and Saulty. The ROD lettering suggests that the photo pre-dates the formation of the WDLR – and the use of French stock helps confirm this. Hunslet No.309 was one of the first batch supplied to France between 10th August and 15th September 1916.

Courtesy Hunslet Archives.

Untitled

Hunslet 4-6-0T taking on water from a well-built tank made up from standard 'Braithwaite' sectional pressed steel panels (a stock RE item) supported on a timber frame. This must be well behind enemy lines given its exposed nature, most likely an interchange yard, as there is standard gauge track visible in the background. Also it has a water feed pipe, possibly from a local water main and even has a level indicator. The loco does not have a water lifter and the broken cab spectacle window shows why later batches were provided with the glass protected with horizontal bars.

Photos: Collection Jim Hawkesworth

BALDWIN LOCOMOTIVE COMPANY 4-6-0T

When it became apparent that Hunslet could not supply their otherwise successful design in anywhere near the quantities required, the MOD started to look elsewhere. Inevitably, all of Britain's locomotive builders were fully occupied, largely with 'War Work' – so the search moved across the Atlantic to the United States of America, still a neutral country and highly industrialised. The Baldwin Locomotive Co., of Philadelphia were quick to offer an adaptation of a 60cm 4–6–0T design already being built for the French Military Railways in Morocco (see photo upper left). These were designated by Baldwin as class 10-12-D. As can be seen, comparing the two photographs on the left, not too much in the way of alterations were required. The new design had a simpler open backed cab and the side tanks were modified but otherwise, the two are very similar.

An initial order for 45 locomotives was placed during March 1916, with delivery promised by October of that year (see photo lower left). No UK builder could offer anything near the unit price of £1,475.00 'FOB New York'[1], resulting in a prompt re-order for no less than another 350 locos (delivered in eight batches during 1916-17) and a further order for another 100 in 1917 – 495 in total. All bar nine, which were lost at sea on their way to France, saw active service.

Compared to the Hunslet 4-6-0T, these were radically different machines and, from the open bar frames upwards, they represented typical Yankee practicality. Whereas UK firms like Hunslet still relied heavily on hand fitting and manufacture of components, large American builders like Baldwin were well advanced with the use of jigs and fixtures, enabling mass production. This de-skilled and

1 – FOB meant 'Free On Board' a common term used by machinery manufacturers and meaning they would to cover the delivery and loading on to a ship of your choice. The customer paid the rest…

Water tank and engine taking water – 7th March 1918
*Three Baldwin 4-6-0T locos numbers 651 & 746 and one unidentified, adjacent to a lineside static
tank mounted on cribbed standard gauge sleepers. The water lifter is being used as the tank does
not have a filler outlet of its own. Looking at the pressure gauges, only 651 seems to be in steam.*

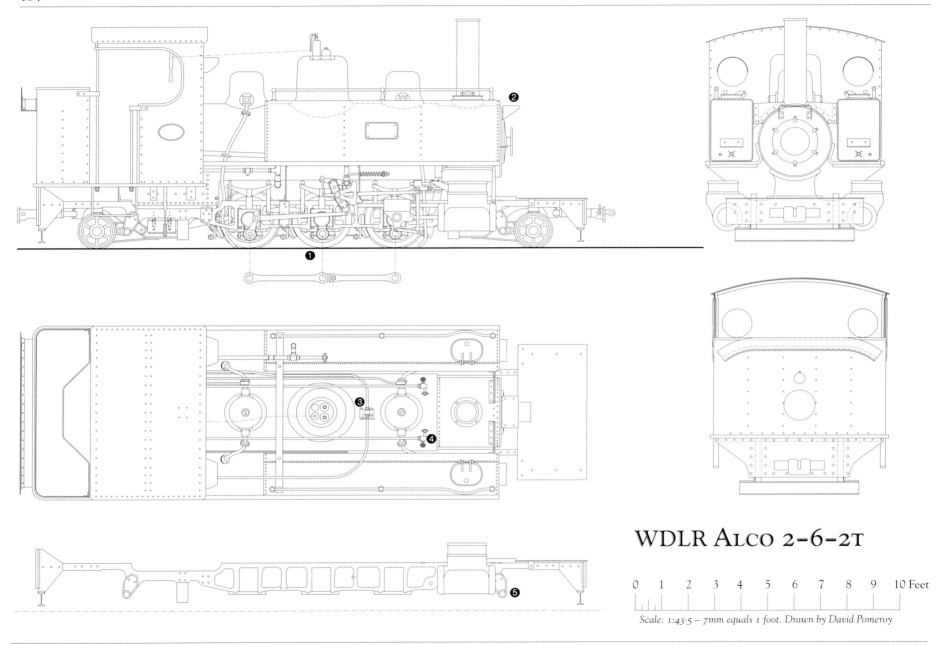

WDLR ALCO 2-6-2T

0   1   2   3   4   5   6   7   8   9   10 Feet

Scale: 1:43·5 – 7mm equals 1 foot. Drawn by David Pomeroy

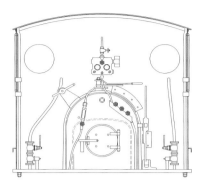

Above: A view of the ALCO backhead, 7mm scale.

Page opposite: The Alco 2-6-2t locomotives as delivered. Coupling rods shown separately for clarity. Important details are:

❶ – *Flangeless centre driving wheels.*
❷ – *Oil headlights omitted, though similar to those fitted to the Baldwin locos.*
❸ – *Injector top feed with shut off.*
❹ – *Injector steam supply valves.*
❺ – *Support pads for bogie control springs.*

ALCO 2-6-2T

With British manufacturers completely tied-up and even Baldwin becoming overwhelmed by demand for the 4-6-0T locomotives they were supplying, the War Office requested a tender from the American Locomotive Corporation (ALCO) for a batch of 100 suitable 60cm locomotives.

They offered a robust 2-6-2T design, with outside frames which became the most powerful of the WDLR steam fleet. Tractive effort at 90% was 6620LBS – greater than the Hunslets or Baldwins. The American Locomotive Corporation was an amalgamation of a number of East Coast builders, these locos being built

Photos: Collection Jim Hawkesworth

Photos: Collection Jim Hawkesworth

by a firm formerly know as Danforth Cooke (New Jersey). Despite now being part of Alco the builder's plates proudly stated 'The Cooke Locomotive Works' – resulting in crews generally referring to them as 'Cookes'.

Quite besides the wheel arrangement, there were plenty of other differences, including a lower set boiler and extra sand pot. Even so, they suffered the toppling problems of the high mounted water tanks in much the same way as the Baldwins, noted earlier. They were rather better fabricated and finished than the Baldwin locos and, like the Hunslets, were popular with Light Railway units, who kept hold of them if they could.

The driving wheels, of 2ft 3ins dia (larger than either the Hunslet or Baldwin locos) were equally spaced on a 5ft 6ins wheelbase. Drive from the horizontally mounted cylinders was to the rear axle and the chassis was fully equalised – in this case including the pony trucks. These latter also had side control springs applied.

The overall length was 22ft 1½ins over couplers, with a total wheelbase of 16ft 6ins. Height to chimney top was 8ft 10½ins and width 6ft 9ins over cylinders. Boiler centre line was 4ft 2ins above rail level.

Above left: Front view of the Alco 2-6-2T showing the way the tanks were braced additionally with two plates fixed to the upper part of the smokebox. Note the drain taps fitted to the front of the tanks – on the Baldwin locos these were at the rear, unlike the Baldwins. There were no front stays, unlike the Baldwins.

Above centre: Rear view, showing the two circular access panels. The lower one aligned with the firebox door – but the purpose of the smaller upper one is unknown. Central on the buffer beam, just under the footplate, is the connection for the lifting injector.
Above Right: The backhead, with typical American fittings. The canister beside the gauge glass is an oil lamp, with rotating cover, allowing the water level to be seen at night. There are also three try cocks. Central, on top of the backhead is a Detroit 'bullseye' lubricator, which fed oil to the cylinders.

Untitled

From left to right are: a pair of Hudson-Hudswell 0-6-0WT locos, an Alco 2-6-2T 'on shed', two Baldwin 4-6-0T locos and finally a lone Hunslet 4-6-0T with another Baldwin barely visible on an adjacent track. The smaller locos were useful for shunting and the larger ones employed hauling long trains from the standard gauge exchange yards on to the forward exchange yards, where internal combustion took smaller trains to the front. See also pages 68-69. The track into the prefabricated loco shed is raised up, so that, inside the locos are supported above ground level in a similar manner to the photo on page 157 – but under cover. See also photo on page 137.

INTERNAL COMBUSTION TRACTORS

The period encompassing World War 1 saw rapid developments with regards to internal combustion – mostly driven by the conflict itself. The smallest design was a 10HP 0-4-0PM unit (below) designed and supplied by McEwan Pratt. Conceived for use on light 9lb per yard rail, these tractors did not perform well in front line conditions and

most were, as a consequence, deployed at rear locations such as Army Workshops. Fortunately though, the War Office soon settled on an innovative design by the Motor Rail & Tramcar Co., Ltd of Bedford.

Mr J D Abbott of Motor Rail, had seen 60cm 'feldbahn' equipment stockpiled quite openly on a visit to Germany prior to the war's outbreak. He was sufficiently concerned that, on his return to England, he and his father set about producing a design of small petrol locomotive, convinced such a device would be useful in any future conflict. This used the 'Dixon-Abbott' gearbox, which the Motor Rail used in their expanding range of self powered tramcars.

A complete specification was drawn up for two designs, 20HP and 40HP, including the superstructure variations of the larger type. This was patented (No.127,399) by Dixon-Abbot and 'another'. There were seven drawings attached to the patent. All aspects of construction were covered and the key features were a strong fabricated chassis, into

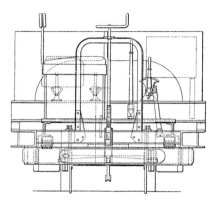

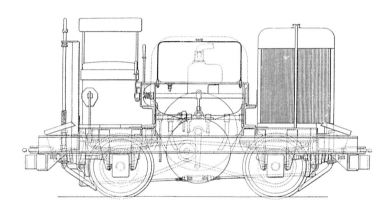

Simplex Petrol Locos.,

Embodying all the principles of high class Steam Locomotives.

20HP Simplex Tractor

The preliminary drawings for the 20hp design. There were some differences between these and the tractors as built. While a few early production tractors had the wide brake stand as shown here, with a 'tramcar' type brake handle (see page 171), most had a much narrower brake stand and spoked wheel.

The 20HP Simplex tractors were easily maintained and all parts were readily accessible. By seating the driver sideways on, a single set of controls was required, probably the first use of what became common practice for small i.c. narrow gauge locomotives. Placing the petrol engine and gearbox transversely in the frames allowed a much simpler transmission to the wheels, dispensing with expensive bevel gearing. While others copied this arrangement later, Motor Rail forever remained the leading producer of the type.

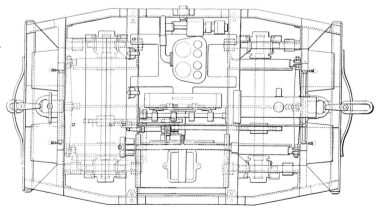

which a transverse engine and gearbox were fitted, driving the wheels through chains. The position of the power unit and drive undoubtedly gave rise to the distinctive lozenge shaped chassis – sometimes referred to either as a 'bow frame' or 'bent frame'.

Initially, while the various war fronts were fluid, the War Office had little interest in light railways. Abbott's approaches regarding light railways worked by petrol tractors fell on deaf ears. In 1914, no less than Lord Kitchener, told Mr T D Abbott with regards to light railways "that is not our way of working".

By 1915, however, the opposing forces were entrenched on the Western Front and the winter of that year saw appalling conditions which stretched supply lines to breaking point. Quite simply, only light railways could link the standard gauge railheads with forward supply dumps and, thence, the front. Experience gained early in 1916, when British forces took over a sector of the front previously held by the French, who had built no less than three light railway systems, convinced the planners that such lines were invaluable. Recalling Mr Abbott and his designs, the War Office, on the advice of their consulting engineers (Messrs Rendell, Palmer & Tritton), placed a trial order with Motor Rail.

20HP SIMPLEX

First in production was the 20HP, 2½ton open tractor, built to a gauge of 60cm. The power unit was a W H Dorman & Co., (Stafford) petrol engine with two cylinders, each 120 mm in diameter by 140mm stroke. The 20 horsepower engines were designed for a maximum speed of 1800 revolutions per minute, and a normal speed of 1000 revolutions per minute, which could be controlled down to 250 revolutions.

Ignition was by means of a Dixie or Thomson Bennett high-tension magneto, provision being made for advancing or retarding the spark by means of a quadrant, placed close by the driver's seat. The carburettor was a Zenith horizontal

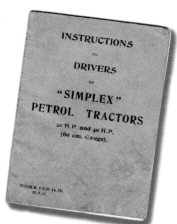

To railwaymen of the steam age, the new 'Simplex' tractors would have been very different to anything they had worked with prior to the war. A small booklet (above, dated 27-7-1917) was printed by the War Office giving a description of both types, with instructions for driving and general care.

20HP SIMPLEX TRACTOR

type. It had two jets, one being for running under working conditions, and the other for easy starting and running at slow speeds. With the throttle of the carburettor nearly closed only the latter was in operation and, as the throttle was opened, it went out of action and the other jet brought into play. The 20HP Simplex carried 14 gallons of petrol, fed by gravity. A combined petrol filter and screw-down tap was fitted between the fuel tap and the carburettor.

The engine drove the patent Dixon-Abbot gearbox (built under license by David Brown & Sons Ltd, Huddersfield) via a foot operated inverted cone clutch with 'Ferodo' lining. The gearbox was a totally self-contained unit and it was this component that made the locos the success they were. Only two levers operated the box. One selected forward or reverse and the other either low gear, neutral or high gear. Apart from one bush, all the shafts ran in roller bearings and, being enclosed in an oil bath, a high degree of reliability was attained. Drive from the gearbox to the axles was via a double chain and sprocket wheels. The axleboxes could be moved in the frames to adjust the chains which, being exposed, were the weakest part of the design.

The 20HP Simplex tractors were easily maintained and all parts were readily accessible. By seating the driver sideways on, a single set of controls was required, probably the first use of what became common practice for small i.c. narrow gauge locomotives. Placing the petrol engine and gearbox transversely in the frames allowed a much simpler transmission to the wheels, dispensing with expensive bevel gearing. While others copied this arrangement later, Motor Rail forever remained the leading producer of the type.

Otherwise the 20HP tractors proved robust and reliable. The first units were tested at Audricq in France and resulted in a stream of orders. Because Motor Rail used a number of outside suppliers (like Dorman's of Stafford who made the petrol engines) production was quite efficient. At the height of war-time demand between 20 to 25 tractors were being made per week, many more than would have been possible if Motor Rail made all the parts themselves.

DRIVING

After turning on the petrol supply (the tank was mounted under the engine cover) the carburettor was flooded, the

ignition turned on and the magneto retarded. With the throttle slightly open the engine was hand cranked to start up. In cold weather the driver was advised to 'drop a little petrol through the compression taps'. Once running, the engine was allowed to warm up for a minute or two then the magneto could be advanced about one third.

After releasing the brakes, the clutch pedal was depressed and low gear selected by pulling the handle towards you. The direction of travel was then selected and the clutch pedal gently let out as the throttle was opened. At full throttle the tractor would be running at around three miles per hour and high gear could be engaged. The clutch was half depressed, the throttle nearly closed and the change speed lever was placed quickly into neutral. Depressing the clutch fully, high speed was engaged and the clutch let out after two or three seconds. While engaging the clutch the throttle was opened up again and advanced to increase speed.

To stop, the throttle was closed, the speed lever placed in neutral and the brake applied. Sand could be applied to the rails from four boxes placed at the ends of the frame. Drivers were advised to 'take advantage of stops to see if the

supply of water in the radiator and fuel in the petrol tank is sufficient'. No doubt the military drivers attended to their own needs as well.

40HP SIMPLEX

By contrast, the 40HP, six ton Simplex tractors, while following the same basic design, were adapted to the rigours of working right up to the front line, if required. For this, three differing body styles were produced; open, protected and armoured.

Production of these larger, more specialised, machines commenced in 1917, the bulk of production being the protected type. Plate steel was used in preference to the channel section outside frames of the 20hp model. Even so, the layout was similar, internally at least, although the driver now sat (still sideways) on the truncated engine cover, instead of beside it.

All three types had curved steel bullet-proof shields at either end protecting the innards. These provided valuable weight for improved traction and, if these were not enough, further ballast weights were fitted under the ends of the frame. Apart from a pillar cab (and roll down canvas side sheets) this is all the protection a driver had with the 'open' version. Shrapnel-proof doors were added to the 'protected' tractor, plus deflecting 'visors' to the cab roof, allowing the driver to look out. The 'armoured' (page 172) tractor has often been compared to a 'little tank' – and rightly so. On all three, the exhaust silencer was on the roof.

The 40 horse-power tractors had four cylinder engines with the same dimensions as the 20HP engines. The 4 cylinder version had a maximum speed of 1500, and a normal speed of 1000 revolutions per minute, which could be controlled down to 250. There were two travelling speeds forward and two reverse, and the speed of the 40 horse-power locomotive was 12·5 miles per hour in high gear, the lowest speed in low gear being one mile per hour. The petrol tank held 20 gallons.

The 'Open' 40HP Simplex tractor (above) offered some protection for the driver, but not as much as the 'Protected' version (below) which had side doors and sloping plates capable of deflecting small arms fire. The radiator was protected from damage by the raised plate on the front right-hand side panel.

Motor Rail – Bedford Engineering

A row of newly built 20HP petrol tractors, led by a single 40hp 'open' 40HP, No.2102. This latter would have been the second of the first batch, ordered in February 1917, the WDLR number sequence being LR2101 to LR2200, all 'open' type apart from six made in 'protected' form. All are in gloss paint, most likely a dark green colour – possibly the 'bronze green' favoured by the British Army for its artillery pieces. In the left foreground are Dixon-Abbot gearbox units, presumed stockpiled, though it seems odd to keep them outdoors.
Collection: John Townsend

EASY ACCESSIBILITY

An outstanding and particularly noticeable feature of the designs of both sizes of locomotive was the manner in which all parts of the mechanism were made readily accessible. This was, possibly, rather more noticeable in the 20HP than in the three types of 40HP tractors, which had more elaborate enclosures.

In the case of the 20HP design, the whole mechanism was protected by a light covering made in two halves, which were hinged in a fore-and-aft direction on the centre line of the vehicle. Each cover could, in turn, be hinged back over its neighbour, so as to lie flat on it. This done, the various parts were readily accessible.

In each type of locomotive a quite comfortable slatted seat was provided for the driver, and from it he had a good view in both forward and backward directions. From it, too, he could reach, without getting up, all the controlling handles and levers, including those for sanding, which were operated by the feet. An individual sand-box was provided for each of the four wheels. All the wheels were braked, the brake blocks being of cast iron and being applied by a hand wheel.

TESTING

For evaluation and testing a circular track, 1·055 miles in length, was made up, comprising a series of continuous reverse curves and including one-third of a mile of 3% gradient. The 40 horse-power locomotive had a fuel consumption of one gallon of petrol to 87·5 ton-miles of useful load, the 20 horse-power locomotive showing 89 ton-miles under the same conditions. The larger engine took 46 tons up the 3 per cent gradient at 3½ miles per hour. The tractive effort of the 40 horse-power locomotive is given as being 3700LBS per ton at 4 miles per hour, and 1350LBS per ton at 9 miles per hour. The table (upper right) shows what the 20 horse-power locomotive were capable of. Both types could negotiate curves as small as 7½ metres radius – say, 24ft 6ins. The table lower right shows the leading particulars of the two sizes of locomotives.

Because of the lack of familiarity with internal combustion engines at the time, a training line, laid out at Longmoor Military Camp in Hampshire, was used to instruct and train officers and NCOs, before going over to France. Nicknamed the 'Scenic Railway' this was a 3½ mile long 60cm gauge system comprising sharp changes in curvature and gradient. Though far better laid and maintained than the track they would encounter 'in the field' this line gave many men, previously unfamiliar with both railways and petrol engines, valuable instruction.

When the war was over, the availability of surplus petrol tractors changed the market for small locomotives considerably. While the 20hp type was most popular, some of the larger 40hp type were also sold. Examples could be found all over the UK, in quarries, factories, water works etc., many still working into the 1960s. Some of these are now preserved and can be seen at various locations, most notably the line at Leighton Buzzard, where many surplus WDLR 20hp and 40hp Simplex tractors worked on lines serving the sand industry.

Gradient	Starting Load on gradient	Low gear 4 mph	Top gear 10mph
4 per cent	11 tons	14 tons	6 tons
3 per cent	13 tons	18 tons	7 tons
2 per cent	18 tons	25 tons	11 tons

SIMPLEX TRACTORS – TABLE OF DIMENSIONS

	20HP Engine	40HP Engine
Length over headstocks	7ft 8ins	9ft 6ins
Length over buffers	8ft 3ins	11ft 1½ins
Width over side plates at centre	4ft 10ins	6ft 6ins
Width over side plates at end	4ft	5ft 6ins
Width over all projections at centre	4ft 10ins	6ft 7½ins
Width over all projections at ends	4ft	5ft. 8ins
Height over shield	–	5ft 8ins
Highest point, excluding shields	4ft 4½ins	5ft 3½ins
Height of platform from top of rail	1ft 8½ins	2ft 6ins
Wheelbase	3ft 6½ins	4ft
Wheel diameter	1ft 5¾ins	1ft 6in.
Journals	5 x 2⅛ins	6 x 2¾ins
Coupling height	1ft 4ins	1ft 4ins
Rail clearance	2⅝in.	3½ins
Centre of gravity above rail	1ft 4ins (approx)	1ft 9ins (approx)
Weight in working order	2¼ tons	6 tons 6 cwt

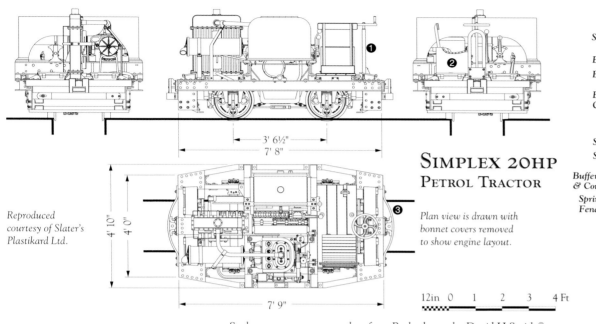

SIMPLEX 20HP
PETROL TRACTOR

Reproduced courtesy of Slater's Plastikard Ltd.

Plan view is drawn with bonnet covers removed to show engine layout.

4' 10"
4' 0"

3' 6½"
7' 8"

7' 9"

12in 0   1   2   3   4 Ft

Scale: 1:43·5 – 7mm equals 1 foot. Both: drawn by David H Smith ©2014.

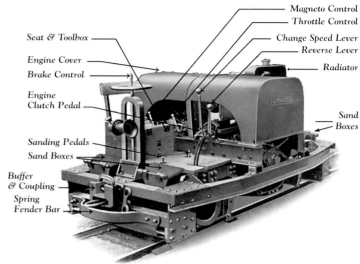

Seat & Toolbox
Engine Cover
Brake Control
Engine Clutch Pedal
Sanding Pedals
Sand Boxes
Buffer & Coupling
Spring Fender Bar

Magneto Control
Throttle Control
Change Speed Lever
Reverse Lever
Radiator
Sand Boxes

❶ – *Brake standard was altered to this form though some early tractors were made as per the Patent drawing, page 168.*
❷ – *The wooden seat also acted as a toolbox.*
❸ – *Horizontal steel buffer.*
❹ – *Maker's plate, see bottom right.*
❺ – *Raised Radiator air intake shield.*

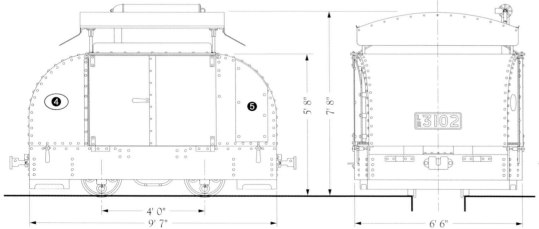

5' 8"
7' 8"

L R 3102

4' 0"
9' 7"

6' 6"

SIMPLEX 40HP PETROL TRACTOR (PROTECTED TYPE)

Throttle Control
Brake Control
Magneto Control
Petrol Tank
Exhaust Silencer
Sand Boxes
Buffer & Coupling

Seat & Toolbox
Reverse Lever
Radiator
Engine Cover
Clutch Pedal
Sanding Pedals
Sand Boxes
Tool Box

MOTOR RAIL & TRAMCAR CO LD
W↑D
SIMPLEX
PATENTS
INDENT No L R 10756
FEB 14 1918
79 LOMBARD ST 1381 LONDON E C

PETROL-ELECTRIC TRACTORS

These intriguing machines were part of 'Programme B', drawn up by the Ministry of Munitions during September 1916. At the time, it was thought that electric powered locomotives might be better suited to work in forward areas than steam locomotives, with their give-away plumes of steam and smoke. To this end, a tender was put out for a total of 200 machines, capable of operating either from overhead wires or independently. In the case of an overhead supply, this formed part of 'Programme B'. However, it was fortunate that the Simplex petrol tractors proved their worth very rapidly, such that notions of catenary reaching towards no-man's land were rendered obsolete.

Even so, the order was pursued, eventually emerging as self contained tractor units, initially at least, made up of 'A+B' pairs. Plans called for one of them to be equipped with a socket to accept a trolley pole for overhead collection. Note though, the Dick, Kerr works drawings do not show this detail – and no photographs show anything of the sort from either builder. There is also no photograph, beyond that on page 176, that shows them coupled as a pair – though some were indeed, initially lettered A or B. The control gear was arranged so that the electric motors could be powered from an external supply, or from the on-board petrol generator set. They could also act as mobile power supplies via built in junction boxes.

British Westinghouse Co., of Trafford Park, Manchester, were awarded the contract for the first 100 tractors and developed the design. While all the electrical components were made by them, they sub-contracted the non-electrical components to other firms. The first 24 petrol engines were

Photo: collection Bob Gratton

1 – This created a problem later, when Nasmyth Wilson, who had fitted their own builder's plates to the body shells, claimed all the locomotives as their own. They did, indeed, build up the first three pairs of tractors in their Patricroft Works, but the remaining 97 of the batch were all finish-assembled by British Westinghouse in an empty factory in Manchester.

supplied by the Tyler Apparatus Company (45HP) and the remainder by W H Dorman (38HP, type 4JO), who were also building engines for Motor Rail. Whole body shells and frame assemblies were supplied by Nasmyth Wilson Ltd[1] (who sub-contracted again to Leeds Forge Co., Ltd) and radiators fabricated by Clayton & Shuttleworth.

A further order for the remaining 100 tractors went to Dick, Kerr & Co., Ltd of Preston, who only contracted out

the engines (Dorman 4JO) and the generator which was made in Bradford by Phoenix Dynamo Manufacturing Ltd. Dick, Kerr provided their own traction motors, which were of the nose-hung pattern, with single reduction gearing.

DESIGN

While the Dick, Kerr tractors were heavier than those made by British Westinghouse (8tons compared to 7½tons),

Page opposite: Works photo of the Leeds Forge built body and chassis, shown bearing a triangular Nasmyth Wilson builders plate. These tractors had more elaborate protection over the cab windows than did those built by Dick, Kerr. Note also the leading sand boxes and panelled side doors.

Right: One of the first three prototype Dick, Kerr PE tractors being prepared in their Preston factory. The substantial nature of both petrol engine and generator (below the petrol tank) is apparent. Note the spring mounted radiator and generally simpler design of the body and chassis. Also the curved spoke 'tramcar pattern' wheels.

Photo: collection Bob Gratton

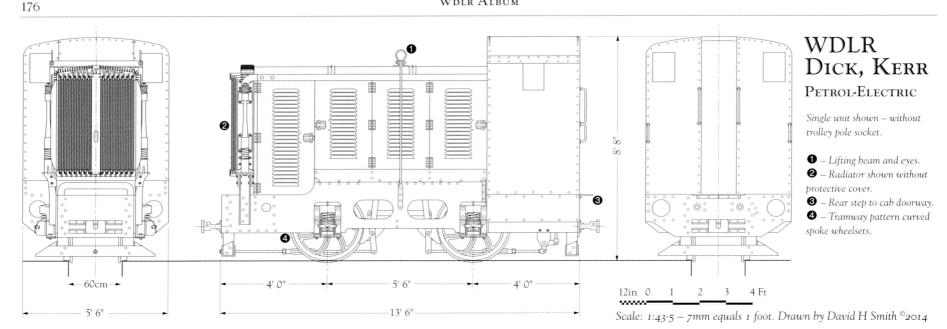

WDLR
DICK, KERR
PETROL-ELECTRIC

Single unit shown – without trolley pole socket.

❶ – *Lifting beam and eyes.*
❷ – *Radiator shown without protective cover.*
❸ – *Rear step to cab doorway.*
❹ – *Tramway pattern curved spoke wheelsets.*

60cm

5' 6"

4' 0"   5' 6"   4' 0"

8' 8"

13' 6"

12in 0 1 2 3 4 Ft

Scale: 1:43·5 – 7mm equals 1 foot. Drawn by David H Smith ©2014

Photo: collection Bob Gratton

Left: An A+B pair in the Works yard of Dick, Kerr Limited, Stoke. These are two of the first three prototypes and have differences from the production run. On the first three, the cab front was cranked around the rear hornguides, but straight on the later ones. Later locos had different pattern horns. The frame width was narrowed on the later ones, resulting in the supports for the radiator being cranked, whereas on the first three, as here, they were straight.

At the left can be seen the early radiator shield, this with a short single row of louvres. Later types would have two full rows, providing a more adequate air flow. The window openings to the cab had simple internal sliding shutters, with horizontal slots. On the production locos, these changed to plain steel sheets. There was no glazing. This is the only known image of a pair coupled back to back as intended.

the designs were very similar, overall. Length was 15ft 1ins, height was 8ft 8ins and width 5ft 6ins. The wheels were 1ft 8ins diameter on a wheelbase of 5ft 6ins.

The two types were easily distinguished by their side panels. While those on the Westinghouse version were plain those on the Dick, Kerr were louvred. In addition, the former had straight spoked wheels and the latter ribbed and curved spokes, like tramcars of the day. Because they were required to act as static power plants, substantial radiators were fitted to maintain the correct engine temperature under load, even when stationary.

The first three were tested on the North Wales Narrow Gauge Railway, at Dinas Junction and, subsequently, at Longmoor, Hampshire, where the War Department had their railway testing and training camp. Once in France it seems that a clerical error resulted in the numbering of the two batches being transposed, the BW locos receiving the DK number series and vice-versa.

In service they were not too popular, the high gearing of the traction motors resulting in them being considered slow, particularly when compared to the steam locos and Simplex tractors. The large petrol engines were also difficult to start, though the ability to connect the dynamo in one loco to the electrical supply from another which was already running meant it could, in effect, be used as a starter motor.

They were well protected against small-arms fire and radiator shields were also provided to prevent coolant loss. The cab windows on the British Westinghouse locos had external sliding shutters, while those on the DK were internal.

The Dick, Kerr locos often carried a pair of long wooden re-railing levers, each with a steel shoe at one end and held in brackets either side of the chassis, atop the horns.

Photos: collection Bob Gratton

Above: The interior of the Dick, Kerr workshops, showing a completed petrol-electric loco suspended over the assembly line. Note the upturned engine housing frames in the lower foreground and cab units behind.

Left: A British Westinghouse PE with the side doors open – the internal arrangement being very similar to that of the Dick, Kerr shown on page 175. This loco lacks its radiator shield, though this may have been removed as part of the work being undertaken. The straight spoke wheelsets are clearly visible, also the lack of ventilating louvres in the door panels. There were though, three large louvres just above the door line, immediately over the engine position.

CREWE TRACTOR

These unusual vehicles were conceived as motive power for the tramways leading directly to the front line, where more conventional locomotives and even patrol tractors could not easily venture due to the very lightweight track. It has been suggested that the daughter of C J Bowen-Cooke, Chief Mechanical Engineer of the LNWR, knew an Army officer who complained of the lack of any means of powered transport for the system of trench tramways leading up to the front lines. As a result, she approached her father, who she thought might be able to offer a solution. The resulting design was ordered under a Motor Transport requisition – not by the WDLR. A total of 132 were delivered to France from late 1916 into 1917.

They were the subject of an article in the technical press of the time which described them thus:

"The subject is a tractor for military purposes of which many have been turned out by the London and North-Western Railway Works. It will be seen that by the use of a few appliances an ordinary motor car chassis is quickly converted into a rail tractor. It will furthermore be observed that all the parts necessary for the conversion are carried by the car itself, so that it may run up to the rails on its own wheels, and there be converted into a locomotive.

The essential parts are the frame members, the rail wheels, and the transmission gear. The frames are of channel section $\frac{5}{32}$ inch high tensile steel plate, shaped

Upper left: The tractor in road form, carrying all the parts required for rail conversion.

Lower left: Converted to 60cm gauge. The road wheels were not kept with the tractors. While the steering wheel was no longer functionable, the column was essential as it carried engine control levers.

Crewe tractor in Ford chassis in 60cm gauge wheels – Undated
Two officers using a Crewe tractor as a rail mounted 'staff car'. For this purpose at least, the tractors were entirely adequate. This example has a Motor Transport number on the bonnet top with its Crewe allocated number on the side. Initially these were 1-132, later altered (as here) with a 0 prefix. Note the spare coupler drawbar in the load tray.

under a hydraulic flanging press, joined at each end by a buffer beam fitted-with a spring central buffer and a cross beam at the centre of two channel sections. The buffers have a link and pin coupling.

CONVERSION TO RAIL

When the motor car is to be converted for use as a tractor, both wheels are taken off the rear axle and replaced by sprocket wheels, with eighteen teeth each which drive, by means of a Hans Renold 1¼in. bush roller chain, on to sprocket wheels, with twenty-four teeth, on the rear axle of the tractor. On this rear axle is another sprocket wheel with twenty-four teeth, which is coupled, by means of a similar chain, to a corresponding wheel on the front axle of the tractor.

The motor car chassis is mounted on this tractor frame, the front axle being secured by U-bolts, as seen in the lower view (page 178), and the rear axle by clips. The latter axle passes through an opening in the sides of the frame, which is made oval to allow for horizontal adjustment of the chains. Inside the opening a steel housing is inserted, which carries an inner and an outer roller bearing. The four wheels of the tractor are of drop forged steel, turned on the tread to the correct gauge and bored to be a driving fit, on the axle. The driving gear on the rear axle is protected by the shield seen in the illustrations, and in front of this is a driving board carried on brackets. The motor car transverse axle springs are retained and reinforced by two spiral springs fixed in a vertical position between the rear buffer beam of the tractor and the underside of the wooden body of the motor car. The driving mechanism is, of course, the same whether the machine is used as a motor car or as a tractor; There are powerful band brakes on the driving axle of the tractor. In addition to the motor car brakes, each of which is applied by a separate lever. The tractor mechanism is efficiently lubricated with solidified grease fed through a spring lock cap grease cup.

The gauge of the tractor is 60cm, The length, over all, is 10ft 4½ins, and the width 3ft 2³⁄₁₆ins, The depth of the framing at the deepest part where the rear axle passes through is 7ins, and it tapers to a depth of 5ins at the rear end, and 3ins at the front end. When on the rail the weight on the front axle is 11cwt 1qtr 26lb, and on the rear axle 10cwt 0qtrs 12lb; total 21cwt 2qtrs 10lb. When on the road and carrying all the tackle for conversion – as seen in one of the illustrations – the weight on the front axle is 8cwt 0qtrs 19lb., and on the rear axle 15cwt 2qtrs 19lb; total 23cwt 3qtrs 10lb.

The engines are of a Treasury rating of 25 horse-power. They are tested on a special trial ground at Crewe, which has a maximum gradient of 1 in 20, and a curvature of 30 metres radius, and the tractor must stop and start again, with a load of 5 tons, on the 1 in 20 gradient. The tractor will haul a load of 5 tons at fifteen miles per hour. It takes about one hour to convert a motor car into a tractor or vice versa.

To enable a tractor to be turned round so as to avoid running on back gear, a self-contained turntable is provided.

It comprises a square-headed screw turning in a nut placed between the two channel sections of the cross beam, and operated by a double pawl ratchet and lever. The car carries a built-up beam, which is placed between the rails, the end resting on the rails. In the centre of this beam is a cup into which the end of the screw enters, and as the ratchet is worked, the car rises until the flanges of the wheels are clear of the rails. The car is then turned and lowered again by operating the ratchet in the opposite direction. Two men can raise, turn and lower a car in three minutes."

The Engineer, October 1918

Although the foregoing sounds encouraging, in practice they were of limited use and the load they could haul (supposedly 5tons) was greatly reduced when running on poorly laid track. Due to the time it took to convert from one mode to the other, most probably spent their days in rail form. However, at the time they were introduced, anything that reduced the back-breaking task of moving ammunition to forward positions was, no doubt, very welcome.

Lack of suitable motive power for forward area tramways and 'Foreways' gave scope for some ingenuity on behalf of the operating troops. Shown here is a lightweight inspection car/tractor fabricated from odds and ends by the Canadian Railway Corps. Nicknamed the 'Mechanical Bug' it used a motorbike engine as a power source, placed in a much modified handcar frame. The operator sat at the rear —as shown here.

The Crewe Tractors were an improvement of sorts, at least . . .

Crewe tractor in Ford chassis in 60cm gauge wheels – Undated
The Royal Garrison Artillery at Elveringhe. Tractor No.39 posed with an improbable load, which must have approached the 5ton capability claimed by the LNWR on test at their works at Crewe. Extra petrol was carried in cans (painted red, and known as 'flimsies') and this example retains the pair of headlights and front mudguard supports – both items which soon got removed from tractors destined never to be returned to road condition. The shells are for a Howitzer (probably 15 inch) and the containers hold the fuses.

CHAPTER SEVEN
ROLLING STOCK
Four Wheel and Bogie Wagons: Ambulance Vans: Workshop Train

 FTER THE WAR OFFICE had decided that a system of 60cm light railways would be required to maintain supplies to the front line in France and Belgium, the provision of suitable rolling stock came under consideration. The initial order for light railway material (Programme A) was placed during March, 1916 and included 1,000 wagons. Initially, these were four wheel designs, later classed as types A and B. Designed with an axle load of just 2½ tons, they were capable of being used on both feeder lines and forward area tramways.

FOUR WHEEL WAGONS CLASS A

These were timber bodied (red deal or pitch pine) on a steel chassis. As originally conceived, they had fixed sides and ends, comprising three planks. Later a modified version

was created, with removable sides and ends – which were interchangeable with those used on the 'c' class bogie wagons. The upper corners were held in place with invert U shaped links, locating in metal brackets. This was supposed

to allow rapid conversion to a flat wagon if traffic required. A third variant had sides and ends only two planks high, with fixed ends and hinged side doors. Later, this design was modified so that the sides could be folded inwards, to make a flat wagon. Provision was also made for fixing vertical stanchions at each corner when so used.

The steel channel chassis were identical on all three, with 1ft 3ins dia cast steel curved spoke wheelsets carried in grease boxes supported on leaf springs. At either end a standard WDLR coupler was fitted in a sprung pocket. On one side only, a brake lever and hanger was provided with a pair of cast iron brake blocks operating on one axle only. Set using a pin, in the manner of standard gauge wagons of the period, the braking was poor, particularly

These illustrations are taken from Robert Hudson catalogue No.101, circa 1920 and show (left) the class 'A' 4w open wagon with removable sides and the class 'C' bogie version (right) using many of the same components. The pin-down brakes, almost at rail level, made them difficult and sometimes dangerous to operate. Note, the coupler shown on both is of a different pattern to that used on the WDLR – though see upper photo on page 189.

RE Working Party – 8th March 1918
The leading vehicle is a class 'C' bogie, followed by an example of the larger class 'D'. Riding over roughly laid and possibly damaged track must have made travelling like this quite difficult – though here the track looks well laid. Note the 'C' class wagon has a small central drop door – a modification made to enable unloading loose material easier.

Photo: Collection the late John Kimber

Right: The 'B' class was produced from late 1916 onwards and had an internal length of 8ft, as opposed to the 6ft of the 'A' class. Width remained the same, though the load, at 3tons 10ct 2qtrs, was identical. It did though, allow the carriage of greater quantities of materials of light or medium weight – see the table on page 192. Sides and ends were detachable, so the wagon could be used as a flat car. This example was built by G R Turner Ltd. Other manufacturers of the type were Robert Hudson Ltd and the Blake Boiler Company.

with heavy loads where the locomotive brakes alone, could not hold the train on a gradient. As the brake, pin and hanger were only 18 inches above rail level, they were awkward to reach and set, even with the wagons standing and near impossible to set while on the move. Later, a ratchet brake hanger replaced the pin down type, making application and release much easier.

CLASS B

An improved version of the 'A' class, similar in design but larger – the internal space being 8ft x 4ft as opposed to 6ft x 4ft. The load remained the same, but the larger body allowed more flexibility. As can be seen in the photograph on this page, the sides and ends were detachable, the sides having two handles for this purpose. Both the sides and ends had stout tapering vertical supports, the lower ends of which located into steel pockets. The upper corners were reinforced in the same manner as earlier wagons with detachable parts. The brake hangers were either pin down or the ratchet type neither of which were really satisfactory. By the time of the photographs in the album were taken (March 1918) these were the most likely 4w wagons to be seen, though largely overtaken by the more versatile bogie types.

CLASS C

The first bogie wagons, with twice the capacity of a standard 'A' class. The bogies were adaptations of the existing steel chassis design. Each bogie was braked on one axle only. Some 'C' class were modified in the field with a central, drop-down door – most likely for unloading ballast or similar. See photo page 183.

With all of the foregoing, a degree of standardisation was attempted but not achieved. A problem rapidly emerged in

that the removable sides and ends were mislaid or damaged. Further, the poor arrangement of the brakes was retained, making the wagons difficult to operate, particularly as they carried heavier loads.

CLASS D

The decision to use heavier rail on most systems meant a larger axle load was feasible, plus experience with the former series of 4w wagons showed the need for versatile

D Class Bogie Wagon

The first 'D' class bogie open wagons were built by the Gloucester Railway Carriage & Wagon Co., Ltd and were completed by December 1916. They had timber underframes and bogies. The load was 9tons 13cwt 0qtrs. While this figure would vary over the various batches and manufacturers, the all timber framed wagons remained the highest. A further distinguishing feature was the number of longitudinal planks forming the doors and ends. Wood framed 'D' class had four planks, steel framed three – though the height remained the same.

Photo: Collection the late John Kimber

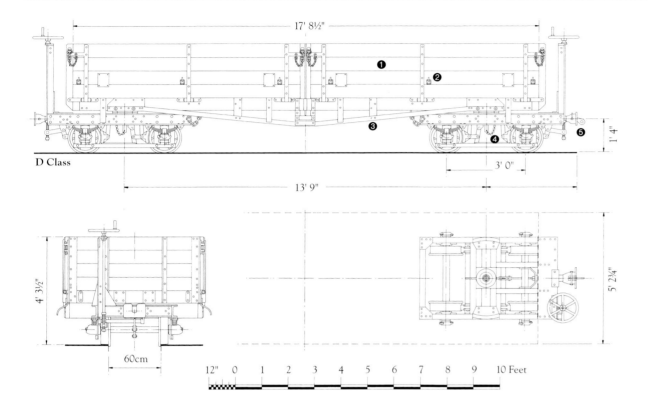

D Class

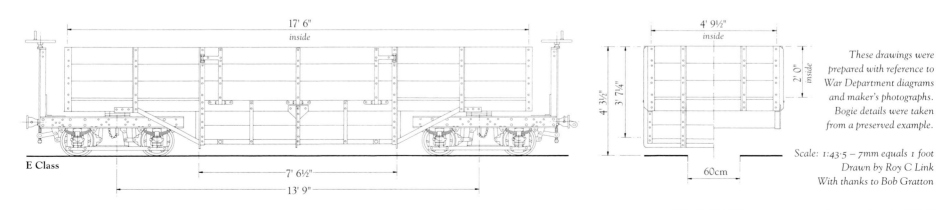

E Class

WDLR D & E Class
Bogie Open Wagons

The drawing top left shows wooden framed 'D' class with steel bogies, as built by the Gloucester Railway, Carriage & Wagon Company Limited, see photo top of page 189.

❶ – *All timber underframe versions of the 'D' class had four plank bodies. The 'E' class had three plank body sides – as did the steel underframe versions of the 'D' class.*

❷ – *Six tie down fixtures were provided per side and one per end, for the purpose of fixing tarpaulins, securing ropes etc.*

❸ – *A distinctive feature of the Gloucester built wagons was the additional gusset plates on the truss bars.*

❹ – *The chain visible between the wheels secured a pin which went through the bogie pivot, securing the bogies in place in the event of a derailment.*

❺ – *The coupling links shown were steel castings, with two slightly elongated holes and formed like a pair of spectacles. Other makers provided a similar link, but forged from round section.*

Note: The 1ft 3ins diameter wheels had seven curved spokes.

These drawings were prepared with reference to War Department diagrams and maker's photographs. Bogie details were taken from a preserved example.

Scale: 1:43·5 – 7mm equals 1 foot
Drawn by Roy C Link
With thanks to Bob Gratton

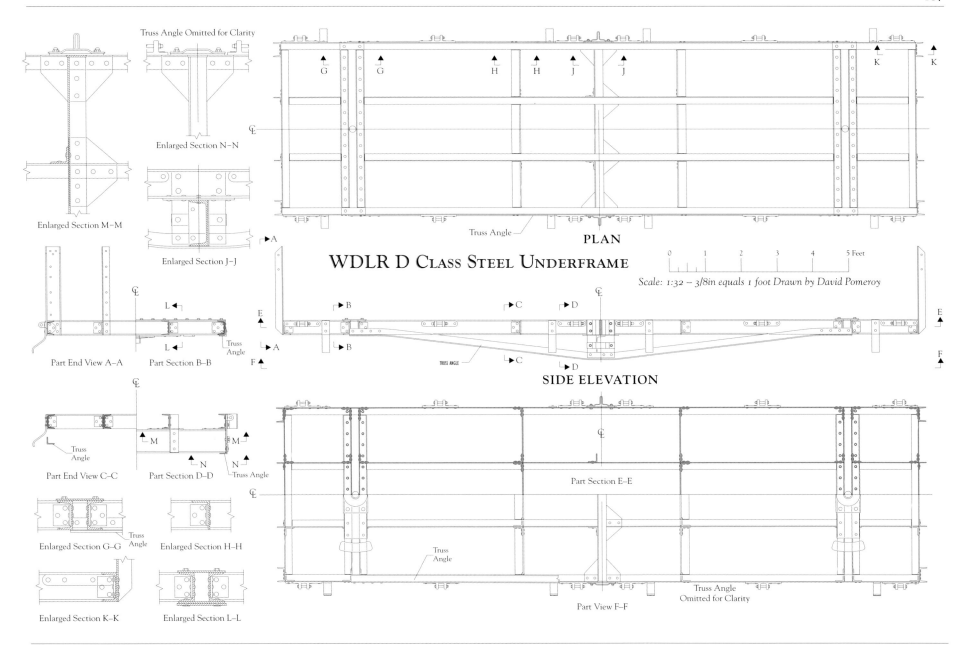

Truss Angle Omitted for Clarity

Enlarged Section N–N

Enlarged Section M–M

Enlarged Section J–J

Truss Angle

PLAN

G G H H J J K K

WDLR D Class Steel Underframe

0 1 2 3 4 5 Feet

Scale: 1:32 – 3/8in equals 1 foot Drawn by David Pomeroy

E B C D E

A

A B TRUSS ANGLE C D F

F

SIDE ELEVATION

Part End View A–A

Part Section B–B

Truss Angle

L L

Part End View C–C

Truss Angle

Part Section D–D

M M

N N

Truss Angle

Part Section E–E

Truss Angle

Enlarged Section G–G

Truss Angle

Enlarged Section H–H

Enlarged Section K–K

Enlarged Section L–L

Truss Angle

Part View F–F

Truss Angle Omitted for Clarity

D Class Bogie Wagon

Photo: Collection the late John Kimber

high-capacity bogie wagons with many interchangeable components. Produced under 'Programme B', which called for a total of 2,800 bogie wagons, the new wagons were designed by War Department consultants, Rendell Palmer & Tritton. The D class open wagon design formed the basis for the E, F and H classes and the bogies were found under other, more specialised types also. It was produced in large quantities by a number of manufacturers so, as a result, there was some variation between them, as a group.

They were capable of carrying a load of up to 10tons, with easy loading and unloading provided by a pair of drop-down doors on each side. The T section centre post on

which the inner ends of the doors latched was removable, so access to the full load bed was unobstructed.

The demands of the war were already affecting the supply of materials, so it was decided that the new design would come in two forms – with steel underframes and bogies and an alternative version with teak underframes and bogies.

In the event, the only 'D' class wagons with a timber underframe and bogies combined, seem to have been produced by just one manufacturer, the Gloucester Railway Carriage and Wagon Company Limited. Those produced by the Bristol Wagon & Carriage Co., Ltd having wooden underframes on steel bogies. In fact, as bogies were produced

Above: Gloucester all timber class 'D' showing the vertical brake wheel that operated four cast iron shoes, one to each of the wheels on the bogie. The side doors, which could not easily be removed, were retained by vertical pins, the doors being protected from damage when dropped by the provision of 'door strikers'. Metal fixtures with loops were provided for tying down tarpaulins.

Page opposite – upper: Gloucester 'D' class with wood body underframe and steel bogies. Dated November 1917, Order No.3590. Note the different pattern couplers.
Lower: Dated November 1918 (order No.3909), this batch had steel underfames and steel bogies. Note the three plank doors and ends. It is very unlikely these vehicles ever reached France, as the war was over and demand for replacements gone.

W ↑ D   TARE 2-10   LOAD 9-10   L.R.6320

War Office.
Bogie Open Wagon with wood underframe & steel bogies
Contract № P.M./ 1896. P.M. 15 №.
Regᵈ № 689 Indent № SALRAIL 237
60 ᶜ/m (1'-11¾) Gauge

W ↑ D   TARE 2-12   LOAD 9-8   L.R.11785

War Office.
Bogie Open Wagon with steel underframe & steel bogies.
Contract. № 23 P/754/ C 995.
Regᵈ. № 1617. Indent № 1TRAIL (LIGHT) 17.
60 ᶜ/m (1'-11⅝) Gauge.

Photos: Collection the late John Kimber

Photos: Collection the late John Kimber

WAR OFFICE.
Bogie Open Wagon with Wood Underframe & Steel Bogies.
Contract No P.M.W 1855 P.M.Le Augt 1917.
Indent No L.R.10449 60% (1·11⅝) Gauge.

Length over Body 17'·8⅝"   Width over Body 5'·2⅞"
Buffers 20'·6⅞"   Sill 5'·10"
Centres of Bogies 15'·9"   Height top of Body to Rail 4'·3½"
Weight 2·13·0

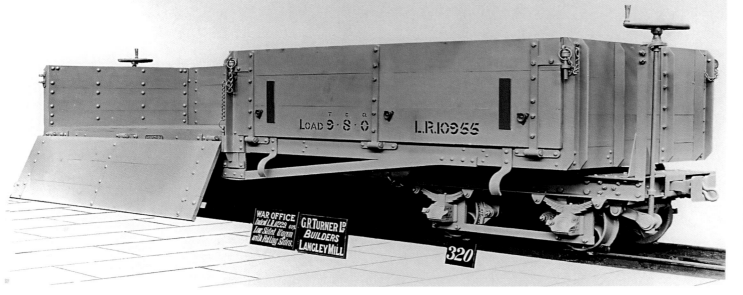

WAR OFFICE
Indent L.R.1229 aeg.
Low Sided Wagon
with Falling Sides.
G.R.TURNER L⁰
BUILDERS
LANGLEY MILL

320

Such was the quantity of 'D' class bogie open wagons required, that no single manufacturer could cope with the demand. In particular, the Gloucester Railway Carriage & Wagon Co., Ltd, was building many other types as well.

Upper: Bristol Wagon & Carriage Works Co., Ltd version of the 'D' class. Timber underframe and steel bogies. No real changes from the later Gloucester wagons. Batch built August 1917.

Left: G R Turner Ltd 'D' class, all steel underframe and bogies. Different door striker shape and tall thin striker plates. One of the few official photos showing one door dropped. Load slightly increased to 9tons 8cwt 0qtrs.

WDLR D Class
Bogie Open Wagons

Upper: Clayton & Shuttleworth 'D' class. All steel underframe and bogies. Raised door striker plates.

Right: Blake Boiler, Wagon & Engineering Co., Ltd 'D' class. Dating from February 16th, 1918, the load is 9tons 9cwt 3qtrs.

Some of these photographs show the wagons in 'Works Grey' livery, used for photographic clarity, to show off the product. When delivered, it is thought that the WDLR wagons were supplied in 'War Office Grey' or 'Battleship Grey' overall– with either white or yellow lettering. There continues to be some debate over the livery.

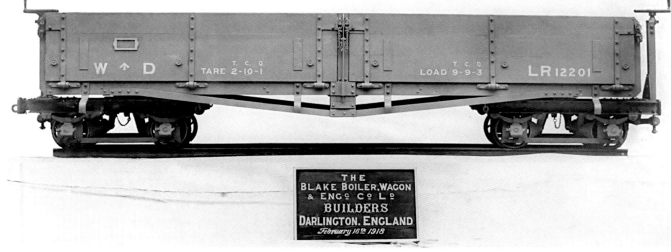

Photos: Collection the late John Kimber

LOADING OF AMMUNITION IN 60cm WAGONS

Nature of Ammunition	6ft Open Box Class A — Load 3½ Tons			8ft Open Box Class B — Load 3½ Tons			12ft Bogie Open Class C — Load 7 Tons			17ft Bogie Open Class D — Load 9¾ Tons		
	Cases	Shells or rounds	Weight Tons	Cases	Shells or rounds	Weight Tons	Cases	Shells or rounds	Weight Tons	Cases	Shells or rounds	Weight Tons
13 Pounder QF	34	136	1·4	48	192	2	70	280	2·75	144	576	5·8
18 Pounder QF	24	96	1·2	36	144	1·9	52	208	2·75	105	420	5·5
60 Pounder Cartridges	16	192	1·1	20	240	1·5	32	384	2·25	60	720	4·4
60 Pounder Shells	—	75	2·1	—	130	3·5	—	200	5·5	—	240	6·75
4·5inch Howitzer Shells	40	80	1·7	56	112	2·4	80	160	3·4	120	240	5·1
6inch Howitzer Shells	—	72	3·2	—	88	3·9	—	140	6·2	—	168	7·5
8inch Howitzer Shells	—	40	3·5	—	40	3·5	—	78	7	—	110	9·75
9·2inch Howitzer Shells	—	26	3·5	—	26	3·5	—	50	7	—	75	9·75
15inch Howitzer Shells	—	7	3·5	—	7	3·5	—	13	7	—	18	9·75
·303 Ammunition	64	—	2·3	80	—	2·8	128	—	4·6	162	—	5·7

LOAD CAPACITY OF WAGONS IN TONS

Material	17ft Bogie Well Class E — 225 cu. ft	17ft Bogie Open Class D — 175 cu. ft	12ft Bogie Open Class C — 122 cu. ft	8ft Open Box Class B — 80 cu. ft	6ft Open Box Class A — 60 cu. ft
Coal	9	7¼	5	3¼	2½
Coke/Charcoal	6¼	5	3½	2¼	1½
Hay	4¼	3¼	2¼	1½	1¼
Oats	7½	6	4	3	2½
Bran	3¾	3	2	1½	1
Ordnance	5½	4¼	3	2	1½
Ammunition	9	7¼	5	3¼	2½
RE Stores: Timber	6½	5	3½	2¼	1¾
Bricks	9	8½	6	4	3
Gravel	9	8½	6	4	3
Rly Material	7½	5¾	4	2¾	2
Posts	2¾	2¼	1½	1	¾
Groceries	6½	5	3½	2¼	1¾
Petrol	5½	4¼	3	2	1½
E F Canteen	4¾	3¾	2½	1¾	1¼

separately to the bodies, it seems likely that wagons were assembled in all manner of permutations. Certainly, the types based on the 'D' class would be found with either steel or timber bogies. In use, the all steel wagons were most likely the more durable.

The new bogie design, either steel or timber framed was a huge step forward with regard to operation. Braking was now on all four wheels but operated by a vertical handwheel supported on a strong bracket on one corner. The bogies also extended beyond the end of the body, providing somewhere for crew to stand if needed. The only drawback was that the brakes on each bogie were quite independent. Thus, on a route with problem gradients, it was not uncommon to see a man positioned between each wagon, having control over two brake wheels, each belonging to two different wagons. While by no means absolutely perfect, this was a huge improvement on the braking arrangements of the 4w wagons.

To keep up with demand, no less than eight manufacturers were involved in their production:

Blake Boiler, Wagon & Engineering Company Limited
Bristol Wagon & Carriage Company Limited
Clayton & Shuttleworth Limited
Cravens Limited
Gloucester Railway Carriage and Wagon Company Limited
Midland Railway Carriage & Wagon Company Limited
Hurst Nelson & Company Limited
G R Turner Limited

CLASS E & F

Essentially, the 'E' type was a 'D' with a dropped centre well between the bogies. The total load was not increased, remaining at just under 9½tons, but the volume available was 50 cubic feet more. Even so, because of the changes, the actual floor area was slightly reduced. The larger volume however, allowed the carriage of greater quantities of bulkier but lighter materials see the tables, above.

Unlike a true well wagon, the solebars did not drop between the bogies but remained as per the 'D' class. Instead an open-topped box was dropped in between the regular floor sections over each bogie. Also, the floor planking was arranged lengthwise – the opposite of the 'D' class. The underframe bracing was altered accordingly and the dropped section was stiffened by three U sections of steel angle.

E Class Bogie Wagon

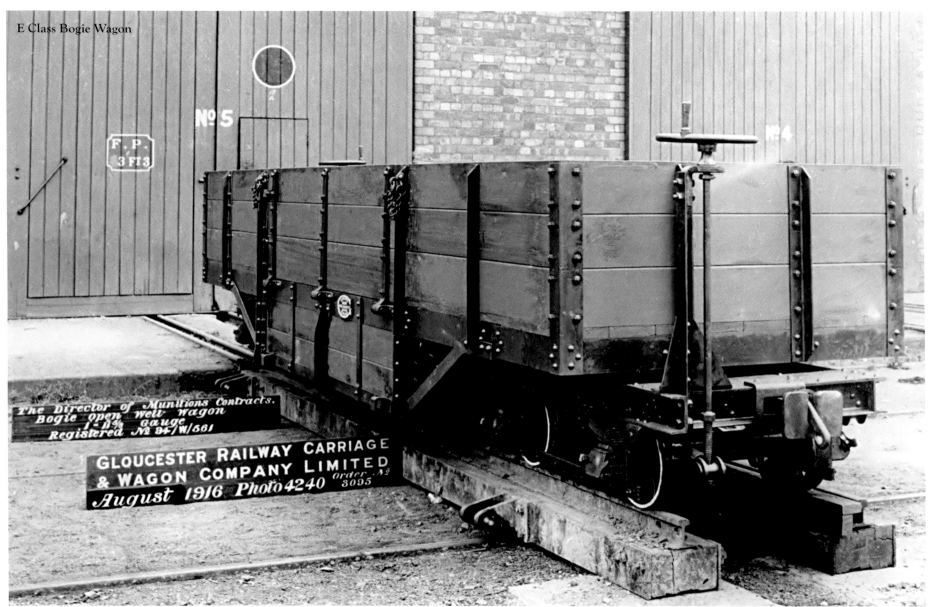

Photo: Collection the late John Kimber

E Class Bogie Wagon

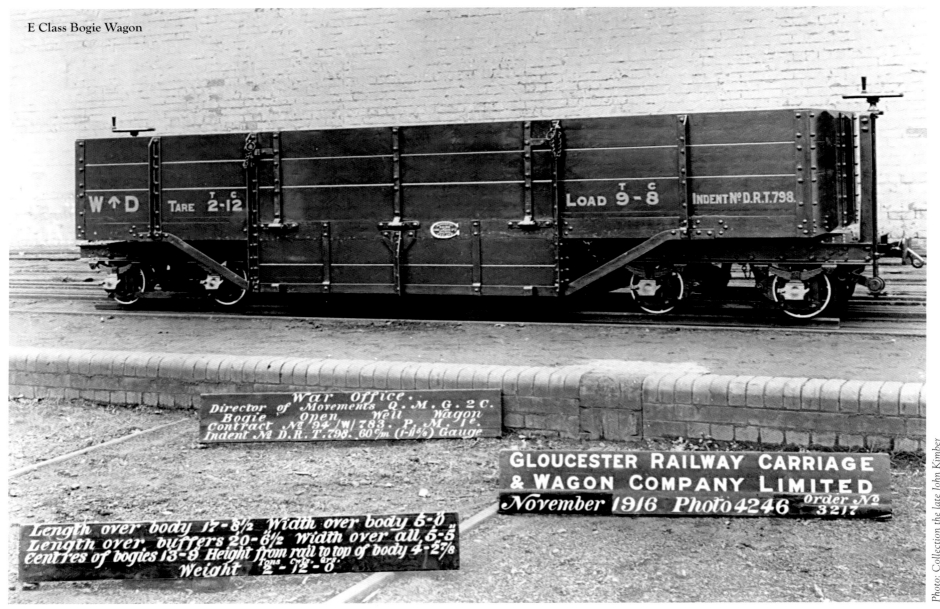

Photo: Collection the late John Kimber

E Class Bogie Wagon
A view showing how the wagons were prepared for shipping to France.
Both bogies are placed inside the body, using custom made timber
packing pieces, one fitting neatly into the well. The brake standards and
wheels were removed and located at one end, so they would not move.

Photo: Collection the late John Kimber

E Class Bogie Wagon

Photo: Collection the late John Kimber

Instead of two doors per side, the 'E' had only one, aligned centrally with the well. This resulted in a vehicle that was more difficult to load and unload – requiring a lot of handling and lifting. While the bodies of both the 'E' and 'F' required steel underframes, there being no timber version, they could be found with either timber or steel framed bogies.

The 'F' class was a derivative of the 'E', having no sides or ends above the solebar. Instead, a series of steel pockets, seven per side and two per end, held vertical stanchions which could be removed if required. They were superficially similar to the French Péchot well wagons, though these latter were all steel and had a much larger 'well'. As with the 'E' class, the 'F' allowed the carriage of bulky loads, though

still under ten tons. An important use for the 'F' class was the carriage of artillery pieces, for which the stanchions were removed and special brackets fitted – see pages 92-98. Once the light railway systems were connected by laterals (see page 78) the relatively easy movement of artillery, up to 18 pound howitzers, greatly facilitated both relocation and recovery.

F Class Bogie Wagon

This example was actually built after the War had ended – for the Andaman Islands, but is otherwise identical to those supplied to the WDLR.

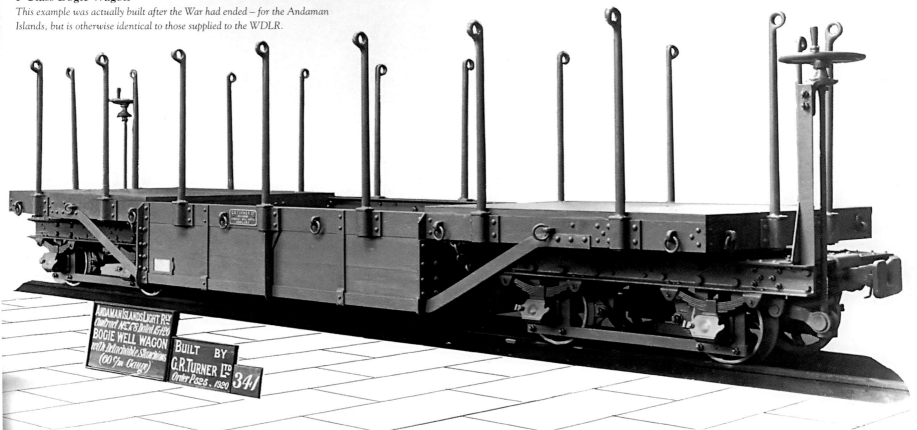

Photo: Collection the late John Kimber

H CLASS TANK WAGON

Given the nature of war, supplies of clean water were often impossible to find, particularly at the front line. Also, supplies of water were required wherever steam locomotives were running. To this end, a bogie tank wagon was designed, using modified 'D' class chassis and bogies. Photographs show only steel underframes and bogies.

The tank, which had a capacity of 1,500 gallons, was a straightforward rectangular shape, formed from riveted steel plates and the makers photographs show that this was zinc galvanised. Once in France they were painted the same grey as all the other 60cm wagons – though some show up in photographs in a camouflage pattern.

At either end was a top mounted lid, big enough for a bucket to be lowered in for filling. Surprisingly, no other form of getting water out was provided – though there were two draining outlets central in the tank base. This compared badly with the French Decauville built bogie tank, which was equipped with a rotary hand pump and two side outlets with taps.

The tank was laid on a timber deck and bolted down

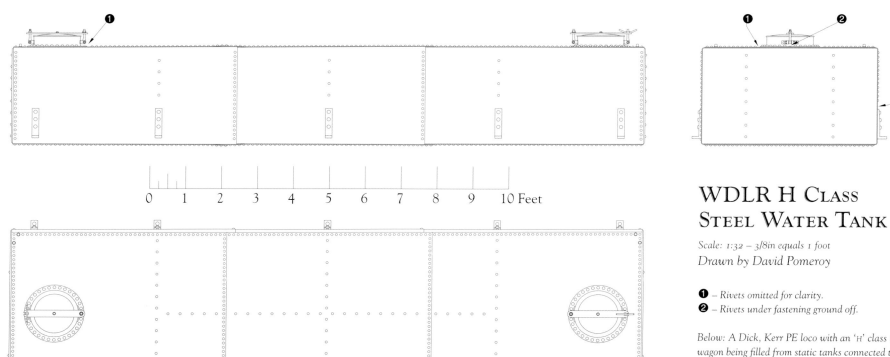

❶

❷

❶

0   1   2   3   4   5   6   7   8   9   10 Feet

WDLR H CLASS STEEL WATER TANK

Scale: 1:32 – 3/8in equals 1 foot
Drawn by David Pomeroy

❶ – *Rivets omitted for clarity.*
❷ – *Rivets under fastening ground off.*

Below: A Dick, Kerr PE loco with an 'H' class tank wagon being filled from static tanks connected to a water main. This must have been clean enough for drinking – note the sign "Fill water bottles here".

H Class Bogie Tank Wagon
The galvanised steel water tank was painted once in
France. Some had simple camouflage.

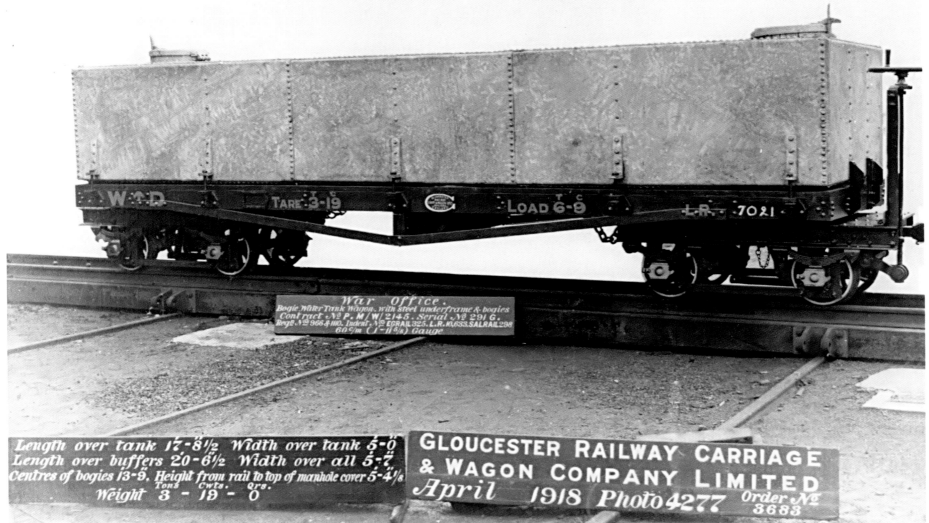

W‸D TARE 3-19 G LOAD 6-9 L.R. 7021

War Office.
Bogie Water Tank Wagon, with steel underframe & bogies
Contract Nº P.M/W 2145. Serial Nº 291 G.
Regⁿ Nº 966 & 110. Indent Nº EGRAIL 325. L.R. 10.633. SALRAIL 298
60 c/m (1'-11⅝'s) Gauge

Length over tank 17-8½ Width over tank 5-0
Length over buffers 20-6½ Width over all 5-7
Centres of bogies 13-9. Height from rail to top of manhole cover 5-4⅛
Weight 3 - 19 - 0

GLOUCESTER RAILWAY CARRIAGE
& WAGON COMPANY LIMITED
April 1918 Photo 4277 Order Nº 3683

Photo: Collection the late John Kimber

H Class Bogie Tank Wagon
Besides the side fixings, there were two upstands at either end to prevent longitudinal movement of the tank in traffic and being shunted.

Photo: Collection the late John Kimber

Workshop Train
Comprised six wagons, seen here in the yard of the Gloucester Railway Carriage & Wagon Co., Ltd.

Photo: Collection the late John Kimber

via side mounted brackets to the underframe. Vertically mounted channel pieces at either end stopped the tank from shifting.

Given that the Hunslet locos took 375 gallons of water, a full 'D' class tank could top up their tanks at least four times. With a tank capacity of 396 gallons, the Baldwins drained them a little faster. Replenishment would, of course, entail a return to base, which could be quite time consuming.

WORKSHOP TRAIN

Of all the series based on the 'D' class bogies and underframe, the Gloucester built 'Workshop Trains' were the most elaborate. Two indents were placed under 'Programme B', one for a train with wooden underframes and bogies, the other for one with steel underframes and bogies. There was no indication as to how many of each type were ordered.

The intention was to provide a completely self-contained mobile workshop, with its own generating system, all electric machinery and electric lighting. Being designed for 60cm track the workshops could be run forward to wherever they were required for speedy repair work being capable of rapid setting up and taking down. Fixed repair depots near the front were increasingly vulnerable to enemy action, being easily spotted from the air. Only heavy repairs, beyond the capacity of the mobile units would thus require sending back to the base workshops.

Comprising six wagons, the train comprised a Generator Car, two Machinery Cars, a Tool Van, Stores Van and Officers Car. Length overall of the whole train was one hundred and twenty three feet, three inches. Each vehicle body was 17ft 8½ins long, 5ft 4¾ins wide, with the roof line 9ft 1ins above rail level.

In use, the generator car and two machinery cars had three horizontally split doors per side. The smaller upper portion hinged upwards, to form an awning and was held by stays. The larger lower portion hinged downward, extending the floor outwards, and had supporting legs and side chains. With both sides let down the total width increased to just over 12ft 9ins. As seen in service, it seems general practice for doors to be opened on one side only. For easy access, wooden stair pieces were provided. In addition, canvas storm curtains fixed along the roof line could be dropped down when the weather was bad. As electric lighting, in the form of ceiling hung shaded lamps, plus portable lights were provided, work could be carried on in most conditions. Livery was described in a contemporary account as "customary War Office grey and lettered in yellow as necessary".

GENERATOR CAR

Positioned at the opposite end to the Officers Car, this contained a pair of petrol-engined DC generator sets, plus an air compressor. The generator sets at either end of the car were by Aster of Wembley with 15/20HP engines driving 10 kilowatt dynamos. Exhaust boxes for the petrol engines were mounted at either end of the roof. The centrally mounted air compressor by Reavell of Ipswich had its own 10HP motor and a large air receiver was positioned under the roof. How air was distributed is not known. Tanks under the frames held water, with petrol for the engines held in

Photo: Collection the late John Kimber

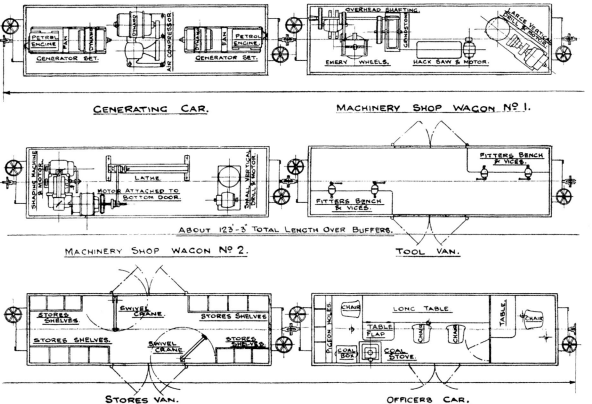

GENERATING CAR.

MACHINERY SHOP WAGON Nº 1.

MACHINERY SHOP WAGON Nº 2.

ABOUT 123'-3" TOTAL LENGTH OVER BUFFERS.

TOOL VAN.

STORES VAN.

OFFICERS CAR.

cylindrical tanks mounted inside the car at either end, the feed being by gravity. Due to the considerable weight of all the machinery the car was blocked up securely at its centre, with additional supports at each corner when in operation. This also served to steady the car, the weight of which was 8tons 9cwt 3qtrs.

At either end, electrical connectors for jumper cables, enabling power to be distributed along the train were fixed just under the roof line. On the Generator Car there were also small doors which allowed the petrol engine starter handles to be inserted. To give room to swing them, the brake standard on the bogies was shortened to provide adequate clearance.

MACHINERY CAR No.1

The first machinery car was equipped with one duplex emery grinder, one 30inch grindstone, one rapid hacksaw, one 1½inch capacity drilling machine. Overhead shafting, powered by a 3HP motor though step-down pulleys, powered the two grinders with the saw and drill each having their own motors. The weight of the car was 4tons 9cwt 3qtrs. The door arrangement, as noted earlier, provided an open working environment with plenty of fresh air!

Generator Car

Shown with side doors closed, note the engine starter handle at the end and shortened brake standard.

W ↑ D   T C Q   TARE 8-9-3

L.R. 4177

War Office.
Director General Railway Materials Branch
Generator Car
Contract № 94/T/1929 Indent № L.R. 10,105
60 c/m (1-11⅝) Gauge

ngth over body 17-8½ Width over body 5-4¾
ngth over buffers 20-6½ Centres of bogies 13-9
Height from rail to top of body 9-1
Weight   Tons Cwts Qrs. 8 - 9 - 3

GLOUCESTER RAILWAY CARRIAGE & WAGON COMPANY LIMITED
April 1917 Photo 4261 Order № 3362

Photo: Collection the late John Kimber

Generator Car

Shown with both sides opened. Note the centre packing and underframe corner supports.

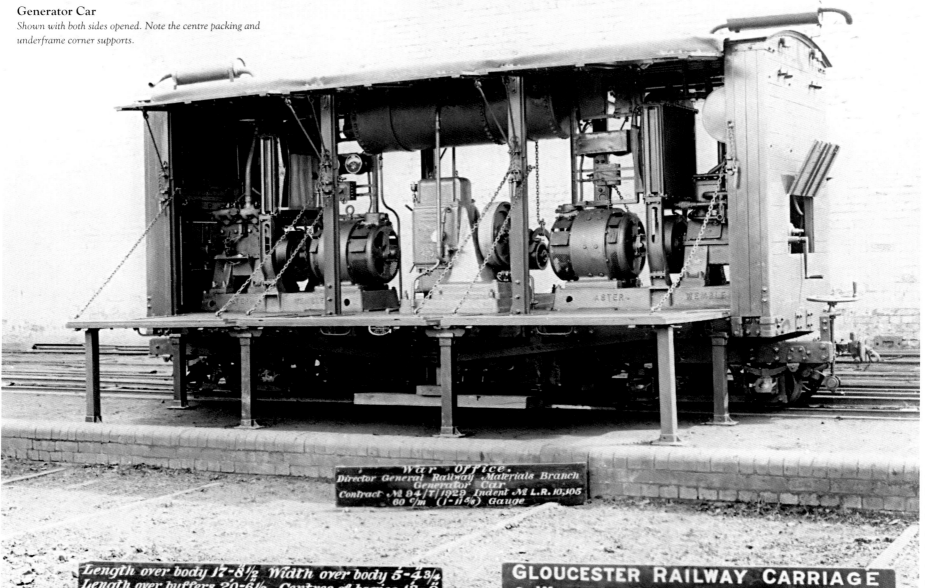

War Office.
Director General Railway Materials Branch
Generator Car
Contract № 94/T/1929 Indent № L.R. 10,105
60 %m (1-11⅝) Gauge

Length over body 17-8½ Width over body 5-4¾
Length over buffers 20-6½ Centres of bogies 13-9
Height from rail to top of body 9-1
Weight Tons Cwts. Qrs.
         8 - 9 - 3.

GLOUCESTER RAILWAY CARRIAGE
& WAGON COMPANY LIMITED
April 1917 Photo 4261 Order № 3362

Photo: Collection the late John Kimber

MACHINERY CAR No.2

This contained more complex machinery, one 8inch shaping machine, one six inch lathe plus a small drilling machine. Drive was similar to Car 1, with overhead line shafting – but the motor for the lathe was fixed to one of the drop down doors, so required connecting by belt to the overhead shafting once the car was set up. In addition, a work stand with vice and a smaller lathe could be mounted on the right hand drop down door – an arrangement that can be seen in the photograph on page 209. To operate this, a belt was run to the shafting used for the pillar drill.

TOOL VAN

Coupled next to the two Machinery Cars, the Tool Van differed in that it had conventional side-hung double doors each side. Inside were fitter's benches and vices, plus drawers and shelving to accommodate hand tools.

STORES VAN

Similar in construction to the Tool Van, this vehicle had a pair of light jib cranes (one per side, capacity unknown) arranged to swing outwards for raising and lowering any heavy equipment that might be required. Along the inner walls were rows of shelves with bins for small parts, nuts, bolts etc. Floor space was occupied with a smith's hearth, anvils and jacks. It was noted in *The Locomotive* (October 1918) that "a useful range of pneumatic tools is carried".

OFFICERS CAR

This was an unusual vehicle, with access via a pair of double doors on one side only, presumably to maximise use of the available space inside. At one end was a small office with desk and chair for the officer-in-charge. The remainder was occupied by a general office with a long table, flap table and bank of pigeon-holes and cupboards. Chairs were provided for three ranking-officers, plus a coal box and stove. An electric heater was provided for the smaller office. The only

Generator Car

End view showing hatch and jumper connectors. Despite the cut down brake handle and support, starting the petrol engine while standing on the projecting end of the wooden bogie would have been a challenge.

Photo: Collection the late John Kimber

car with side windows, it represented the closest anything built for the WDLR got to being an actual coach.

Any permutation of the vehicles comprising the full train could be operated without the Generator Car if hauled by one of the Petrol Electric locos – as these would be capable of operating as a generator set to provide power. When set up at a depot the train would also be used to supply electric power to other equipment.

Machinery Car No.1
Doors closed in travelling condition.

W↑D TARE 4-19-3

L.R. 4179

War Office.
Director General Railway Materials Branch
Machinery Car No 1
Contract No 94 T 1928 Indent No L.R. 10,105
60 c/m (1-11½") Gauge

Length over body 17-8½ Width over body 5-4¾
Length over buffers 20-6½ Centres of bogies 13-9
Height from rail to top of body 9-1
Weight Tons Cwts. Qrs.
4 - 19 - 3

GLOUCESTER RAILWAY CARRIAGE
& WAGON COMPANY LIMITED
March 1917 Photo 4255 Order No 3362

Photo: Collection the late John Kimber

Machinery Car No.1
Doors open, set up for operation. Note ceramic fuses on fuse board, left.

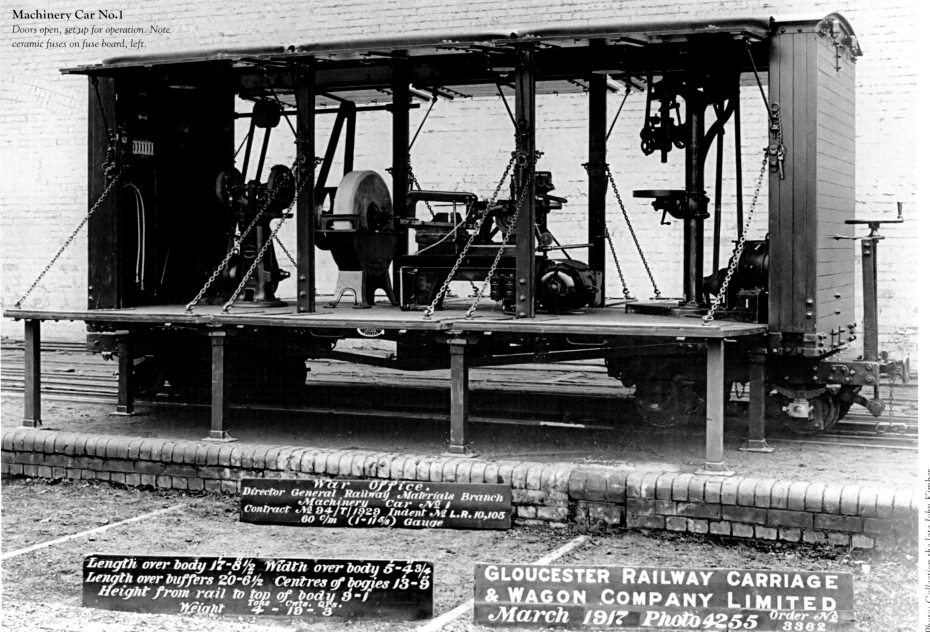

War Office.
Director General Railway Materials Branch
Machinery Car № 1
Contract № 94/T/1929 Indent № L.R. 10,105
60 ⁰/m (1-11⅝) Gauge

Length over body 17-8½ Width over body 5-4¾
Length over buffers 20-6½ Centres of bogies 13-9
Height from rail to top of body 9-1
                    Tons Cwts. Qrs.
Weight   4 - 19 - 3

GLOUCESTER RAILWAY CARRIAGE
& WAGON COMPANY LIMITED
March 1917 Photo 4255 Order № 3362

Photo: Collection the late John Kimber

Machinery Car No.2
Doors open, set up for operation.

Photo: Collection the late John Kimber

Untitled
A Workshop train 'somewhere in France' showing the second machinery wagon, with the smaller of two lathes mounted on the nearest drop-down door. Note the additional timber support directly underneath for reinforcement. There is a strategically placed fire bucket placed beneath the dropped door.

Tool Van

War Office.
Breakdown Van.
Contract № P.M/V/291. Reg№ № 1009.
60 %m (1-11⅝) Gauge.

These vans are same as supplied under Indent №
10,183. except that bogies are of steel.

Length over body 17-8½ Width over body 5-4¾
Length over buffers 20-6½ Centres of bogies 13-9
Height from rail to top of body 9-1
Weight 3-4-0

GLOUCESTER RAILWAY CARRIAGE
& WAGON COMPANY LIMITED
January 1918 Photo 4273 Order № 3717

Photo: Collection the late John Kimber

Stores Van

War Office.
Director General Railway Materials Branch
Stores Van
Contract № 94/T/1929 Indent № L.R. 10,105
60 c/m (1-11⅝) Gauge

Length over body 17-8½ Width over body 5-4¾
Length over buffers 20-6½ Centres of bogies 13-9
Height from rail to top of body 9-1
Weight 4 - 2 - 2

GLOUCESTER RAILWAY CARRIAGE
& WAGON COMPANY LIMITED
March 1917 Photo 4254 Order № 3362

Photo: Collection the late John Kimber

Officers Car

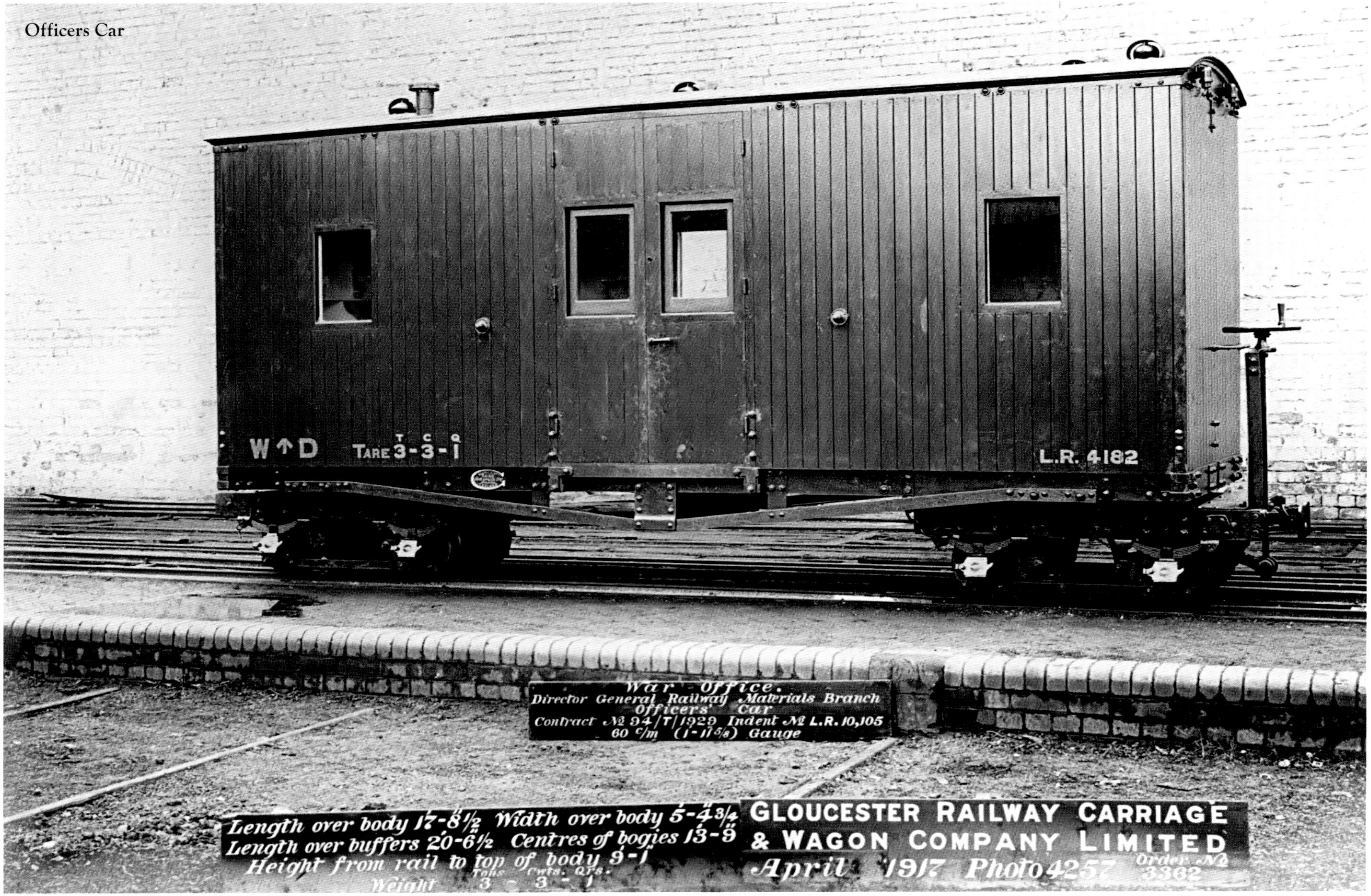

War Office.
Director General Railway Materials Branch
Officers' Car
Contract №94/T/1929 Indent №L.R.10,105
60 c/m (1·11⅝) Gauge

Length over body 17-8½ Width over body 5-4¾
Length over buffers 20-6½ Centres of bogies 13-9
Height from rail to top of body 9-1
Weight 3 - 3 - 1 Tons Cwts. Qrs.

GLOUCESTER RAILWAY CARRIAGE
& WAGON COMPANY LIMITED
April 1917 Photo 4257 Order №3362

W↑D TARE 3-3-1   L.R. 4182

Photo: Collection the late John Kimber

Officers Car

Interior view, looking towards pigeonholes and cupboards. Coal stove at left. Note fixed electric light and shaded light on flex, for lowering over the table area. At the lower right is an electric heater.

Photo: Collection the late John Kimber

BOGIE AMBULANCE VAN

Some time in 1917, under 'Programme B', an order was placed for the provision of "covered goods wagons with ambulance fittings".

Unlike the previous bogie wagons, all of which were based on the 'D' class underframe, this vehicle was longer, with a fixed wheelbase of 16ft 6in as opposed to 13ft 9in. The body (pitch pine frame with red deal boards and elm floor), was much larger than anything else, at 20ft 6in long, 6ft wide and with an internal headroom of 6ft 3in. As a result the steel underframe was a new design though standard steel bogies were fitted. On either side a pair of top hung sliding doors opened to reveal a generous 7ft wide opening. Narrow sliding doors were provided at the ends also, allowing the attendants to move between wagons and access to the external hand operated brake wheels.

Internally, there were six sets of folding brackets to hold stretchers on one side of the doors, and three only on the other side making a total of nine. On the remaining internal wall there was a fold down bench which, at a pinch, could seat up to four 'walking wounded'. Above the bench were a further pair of stretcher brackets, though these were not generally used. With neither windows nor ventilators, travel must have been unpleasant and, if in one of the upper stretcher positions, claustrophobic. Possibly the end doors were opened to allow a through flow of air, but this would have brought in dust etc. There are, though, some photographs taken in France which show small opening windows, centrally high up in each side wall. Presumably a field modification.

The wagons seem not to have been deployed for carrying goods, as no doubt, it was found that their high centre of gravity made them unstable when loaded. As a result, they were put to their secondary purpose as 'ambulance vans'. This involved moving the wounded from forward areas back to the nearest Clearing Hospital. Besides their use to move the wounded away from the front, they were also used

Photos: Collection the late John Kimber

Covered Van (Ambulance)

W↑D

TARE T/C 3-12   LOAD T/C 8-8   L.R.7997

War Office.
Bogie Covered Goods Wagon (Ambulance)
60 c/m Gauge (1-11⁵/₈)
Contract Nº P.M/W.2330. Regᵈ Nº 1172.
Indent Nº L.R.10.741.

Length over corner pillars 20-6   Width over pillars 6-0
Length over buffers 23-3½   Width over roof 6-4½
Centres of bogies 16-6   Height from rail to top of roof 8-6³/₈
Weight   Tons 3   Cwts 12   Qrs 0

GLOUCESTER RAILWAY CARRIAGE
& WAGON COMPANY LIMITED
May 1918 Photo 4279   Order Nº

Photo: Collection the late John Kimber

Covered Van (Ambulance)

A full compliment of stretchers and 'injured' in place. While all the positions offered only basic comfort, travelling on the upper tier must have been very unpleasant. Possibly this accounts for some vehicles being modified with small windows, high up on the sides.

Photo: Collection the late John Kimber

at Trouville. In February 1918, a military complex, known as the 'Trouville Hospital Area' was established near to Le Havre. It comprised no less than three large General Hospitals (72nd, 73rd and 74th) and three Convalescent Depots (13th, 14th and 15th). The latter were a new idea and each could hold 5000 men. Their purpose was to allow

casualties, not so seriously wounded as to require returning to the UK, to recover before being sent back to duty.

The chosen site was some two miles and 300ft higher than the nearest mainline station and, as the local roads were poor, a 60cm line was laid, on a 1 in 50 gradient. Intended for the conveyance of materials for constructing

the site and buildings, it was retained for moving the wounded and connecting the Hospitals and Depots. The Ambulance Vans, running on well laid track at last, were found particularly useful. The system eventually consisted of some 5½ miles in total.

SPECIAL PURPOSE FOUR WHEEL WAGONS

In addition to the foregoing wagons for general service, there were other classes produced for more specific purposes. These were classes, G, K, L, M, & P.

CLASS G

Using a standard class 'A' underframe, these wagons comprised three upright riveted tanks, each containing around 180 gallons of fluid, in order – paraffin, cylinder oil and lubricating oil. They were intended for use in depots servicing the petrol tractors and were not manufactured in large quantities.

CLASS K

For construction and clearing work, a large number of side tipping skips were ordered. Supplied by Robert Hudson Ltd (18 cubic ft capacity) and McLachlan Ltd (27 cubic ft capacity) they were typical civilian products of the day and pretty much 'off the shelf' designs in no way specially adapted for military service. A rake of the 27 cubic ft type can be seen in the photograph on page 69. Two of these are braked and two of the skip bodies have riveted 'feet' on either side so the body can be lifted off and set down without falling on one side. Chassis are made up from steel channel, with axleboxes bolted on directly. The smaller 18 cubic ft Hudson type had steel channel side frames with pressed metal chassis ends. Both supported the skip with invert V steel channel at either end. Neither type had standard WDLR couplers and retained the simple pattern common to such products.

CLASS L

When war work threatened to swamp British manufacturers during 1916, the need for more tipping wagons resulted in a trial order for wagons from America. In the event, makers in the UK rose to the challenge, but a small number of US pattern either-side tipping wagons made by the Western

A long train of Robert Hudson side tipping skips in the charge of a 20HP Simplex tractor. Travelling in the loose bucket bodies, on unsprung chassis might have saved leg muscles, but could hardly have been comfortable. This photograph was used as the basis for one of the 'War Bond' postcards, though the rendering was quite crude.

PAVING THE WAY FOR THE GUNS.

Wheeled Scraper Company of Aurora, Illinois, did reach France for use of the WDLR.

They were quite unlike the UK tippers, having oak bodies mounted high up on three central pivots on a central spine and retained by chains at each corner. Being inherently unstable when loaded, tipping was achieved by slipping the chains on one side. A system of levers on each end, fixed to the doors and sub frame, ensured that, as the body tipped the door on that side was lifted clear, releasing the load. Either door could be lifted independently, even if the body remained level, thus allowing the load to be shovelled on or off. The bodies had a capacity of 40 cubic feet. Identical wagons were supplied to the American Expeditionary Force Railway Companies serving in France.

M CLASS

Great thought was given to how to ease delivery of munitions and supplies over the last few hundred yards, one solution being easily laid down monorails. The class 'M' monorail trucks were built in large quantities (just over 1,400), some by the Gloucester Railway Carriage & Wagon Co. Ltd (see overleaf). Designed to run over 9LB per yard rail, the maximum load that could be transported

Photo: Collection the late John Kimber

Above: Gloucester class 'M' monorail truck with cross pole in place. Left: Class 'L' wooden tip wagon in use moving surplus material as part of a yard is extended. The two horses are pulling a scraper, to level the ground, prior to track laying. Note the gun carriers in the background.

WDLR L CLASS
WOODEN TIP WAGON

The wooden 'L' class side tipping wagons were built in the USA by the Western Wheeled Scraper Co.

❶ – *Side chains at each corner secured the tipping body. If the chains on one side were released, the body would tip away from the operator.*

❷ – *Side doors were lifted up as the body tipped by a system of levers.*

❸ – *Couplers were 'link & pin' pattern, there is no evidence that the standard WDLR type were ever fitted.*

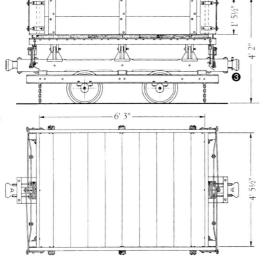

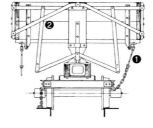

These drawings were prepared with reference to War Department diagrams and maker's photographs. Scale: 1:43.5 – 7mm equals 1 foot Drawn by Stuart L Baker

12in   1   2   3   4 feet

was 10cwt. To achieve propulsion and balance, a vertical support at one end held a horizontal length of steel piping, six foot long, allowing a man to stand either side and push the truck along. When stationary, the pipe, which was held by chain, was removed, the truck tilting over to one side to rest on a skid mounted under the framing. Imbalance was simply achieved by placing the two 10inch diameter wheels an inch or so off the centre line. The 9inch high lattice sides were detachable, though the ends were fixed.

CLASS N

Only a small number of these hopper type 4w wagons were provided, probably by Robert Hudson Ltd. They were typical civilian industrial gable-bottom side-discharge hopper wagons, most useful in distributing ballast when tracklaying. Of all steel construction, the upper sides were

P Class Ration Wagon

fixed, with lengthwise doors beneath, hinged at their tops. These latter were operated by a system of levers at either end, allowing complete discharge of the contents, the floor being a longitudinal inverted V shape. The inside body dimensions were 6ft 9in long by 4ft 0ins wide and 2ft 6ins deep. They had 12inch diameter wheels on a 3ft 6inch wheelbase.

CLASS P

From the middle of 1917 these wagons were produced for operation over the light forward tramways. A stipulation on the design was that they would be light enough for animal or human traction, but strong enough to be hauled by petrol tractors (up to 40HP) on the main 60cm rail system. This solved the problem of shipping a load from one wagon to another, speeding up supplies to the trenches. Like many of the other classes, they were produced by a number of different manufacturers, six in total.

The chassis was all steel with coil sprung axleboxes and standard pattern coupler. A drawback was the lever and ratchet handbrake, operating on one wheel only, continuing the braking problems of the earlier four wheel wagon designs. Tie-down rings for ropes were provided on the sides and ends of the steel frame and some wagons were supplied complete with tarpaulins.

Photos: Collection the late John Kimber

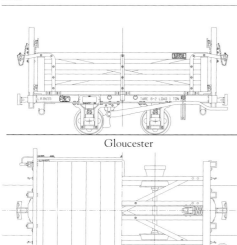

Gloucester

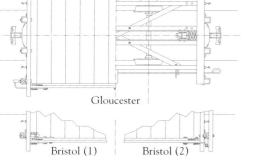

Gloucester

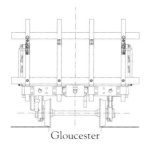

Gloucester

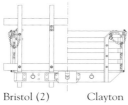

Bristol (2)

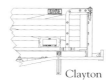

Clayton

Clayton

Bristol (1)   Bristol (2)

0 1 2 3 4 5 6 7 8 Feet

WDLR P CLASS RATION WAGON

Scale: 1:43.5 –
7mm equals 1 foot
Drawn by John Townsend

NOT TO BE LOADED WITH
MORE THAN ONE TON AND
NOT TO BE RUN IN TRAINS
HAULED BY ANY POWER
GREATER THAN 40HP TRACTOR

WD
B.W.&C.W Cº Lᵀᴰ   1918

THE
BRISTOL WAGON & CARRIAGE
WORKS Cº Lᵀᴰ
BUILDERS
1918
BRISTOL ENGLAND

Above: The 'P' class wagons were particularly useful in moving injured soldiers classed as 'walking wounded' away from the front, as this scene shows.

The Bristol built version had upper end beams for carrying stretcher cases, though note only one beam was removable, which made placing the two lower stretchers in place, harder than it need be.

Photos: Collection the late John Kimber

P Class Ration Wagon

In this form four stretchers could be carried, two over two. The upper cross beams being removable to allow the lower pair of stretchers (with injured men) to be lowered in place onto the cross beams, before the upper pair were located on the replaced upper cross members. The sides would be lowered while this was undertaken.

GLOUCESTER RAILWAY CARRIAGE & WAGON COMPANY LIMITED
August 1918 Photo 4282 Order No 3798

War Office.
Wheeled Ration Wagon with steel underframes
60 c/m Gauge (1-11 5/8)
Contract No P.M/W/2394.   Regn No 1257.
Indent No L.R. 10,766.

Length over headstocks 6-8 Width over headstocks 4-0
Length over buffers 7-11¼ Width over all 4-10
Wheelbase 2-6   Wheels 1-0 dia on tread
Weight Cwts. 8 Qrs. 2

Photo: Collection the late John Kimber

P Class Ration Wagon

These wagons carried plates, warning against "loading with more than one ton" and advising they "should not be run in trains hauled by any power greater than a 40hp tractor".

WAR OFFICE
Indent L.R. 10765
60 c/m Ration Wagons
With ends to Carry Stretchers
(With Side Doors)

G.R.TURNER Lᵗᵈ
BUILDERS
LANGLEY MILL

314

WAR OFFICE
Indent L.R. 10765
60 c/m Ration Wagons
With ends to Carry Stretchers
(Without Side Doors)

Photo: Collection the late John Kimber

Bodies were timber, initially with timber lattice drop-down sides and fixed ends. Later batches changed to taller 'lift-off' ends, fixed into side pockets on the chassis. The side doors remained the same. Where wagons were specified to carry stretchers, the ends had an upper bar, which would support two stretchers, side by side. Looking at photographs, the top bars were either fixed or removable, depending on the manufacturer.

Indent No.10765 called for wagons with sides doors and ends suitable for carrying stretchers, as well as wagons with no side doors (see photo above). In the latter case, the door fittings seem to have been retained.

BOGIE FOR GUN TRUCKS

As may be noted on page 93, the vertically mounted brake on the standard WDLR bogie had to be removed when using an 'F' class wagon to carry artillery pieces. To solve this, and to provide bogies for the other pattern of gun carrier seen on page 218, a version of the bogie was produced with a horizontal brake, with the operating wheel below the bolster level. This was positioned under the frames at one end angled slightly outwards, making the brake wheel a little more accessible. While the wheelbase was the same as the standard steel bogie, only one axle was braked. See photograph page opposite.

WDLR COUPLINGS

As noted on page 4, the choice of 60cm gauge was influenced by the existing equipment already in use on the Western Front. Similar pragmatism was exhibited in the choice of coupling, a pattern compatible with that fitted to the

Photo: Collection the late John Kimber

Above: A pair of couplers with 'C' pins – that on the left showing how the pivot was arranged. See also page 95.

Below: The coupler on the left has a 'C' pin clip, that on the right the simpler version with a 'French' pin. Both types of pin were retained by chains to the wagon bodies.

French Péchot equipment being adopted, see photograph on page 154 showing a Hunslet loco with a train of French bogie wagons. Essentially, they were a 'link & pin' pattern coupling, turned through 90 degrees.

The WDLR version had a rectangular buffing face with an upper vertical slot, the space behind being slotted also. Vehicles were coupled using a 'spectacle' shaped link, with two holes held in place by a horizontally placed pin through the coupler body. Some were solid, but others were forged from round section. In the case of the solid 'plate' links the coupler castings had a lug on the underside with a chain to retain the link so they were not lost.

The pins securing the links required retaining, being horizontal, to prevent them coming out when in motion. A common method used by the various manufacturers was an arched loop, pivoted in a slot at one end, and passing over the coupler body, clipping on to the other end of the pin, so securing it. A simpler alternative was a pin with a hinged section, known as a 'French' pin – that had to be lifted to align with the hole in the coupler body, before the pin

A similar form,
showing the 'c' type pin retainer clearly.

could be removed. The coupler shank passed through the wagon headstock and was retained by a substantial spring which provided buffing in tension and compression, plus a degree of articulation.

Wagon damaged by shell fire – 7th March 1918

This 'D' class shows the sort of damage that the WDLR stock was sometimes subject to. Despite the caption in the Album, it is just possible this wagon was being used for light artillery practice, as it is on a steep gradient – which would allow it to be hauled up and allowed to run down unaided, to provide a moving target.

APPENDICES

HUDSON WELL TANK ENGINE TYPE 0·4·0 CLASS 8

HUDSON WELL TANK ENGINE TYPE 0·6·0 CLASS 4

SCALE 3/16"   TONS 1·8 - 1·8 - 2·175   TOTAL WEIGHT EMPTY   TONS 5·755
2·2125 - 2·2875 - 2·3875   "   "   WKG ORDER " 6·8875

CONTEMPORARY DIAGRAMS & TABLES

To help light railway operating troops familiarise themselves with the locomotives and stock of the 60cm lines, a small pocket book was provided in 1917, made up from blueprint sheets, stapled together. Besides the diagrams that appear on the following pages, there were useful tables, which have been re-set for clarity. The information provided would have been of particular use to railway operating troops from Australia and Canada, who were very active in Flanders from 1916 onwards. Later, American troops would also find the booklet essential.

The diagrams, all originally drawn to a constant scale of 1:64, provided a recognisable outline of each item, plus overall dimensions, weights etc. Assembling a full set of diagrams has proved difficult, and those shown here are from a variety of sources, though most come from copies in the collection of the late John Kimber plus a few held by the Australian War Memorial. The latter are reproduced by kind permission of Dr Roger Lee, Head of the Australian Army History Unit. As the format is varied, all are reproduced as black line for clarity – not as blueprint copies. It may well be that each railway operating troop assembled their own version, containing appropriate diagrams only, not all of those available.

BARCLAY WELL TANK ENGINE TYPE 0·6·0 CLASS 5

TONS   1·75   1·57   1·8   TOTAL WEIGHT EMPTY   TONS 5·12
"   2·2   2·1   2·05   "   " IN WKG ORDER · 6·37

Collection: the late John Kimber & Australian Army History Unit

DETAILS OF 60cm LOCOMOTIVES

	Hudson 0-6-0 Well Tank	Barclay 0-6-0 Well Tank	Hunslet 4-6-0 Side Tank	Baldwin 4-6-0 Side Tank	American 2-6-2 Side Tank
Cylinder diameter	6½ins	6¾ins	9½ins	9ins	9ins
Cylinder stroke	12ins	10ins	12ins	12ins	14ins
Boiler length	5ft 6ins	5ft 10ins	5ft	7ft	–
Boiler diameter	2ft 1inch	2ft 2¾ins	2ft 9ins	2ft 9ins	2ft 8ins
Coupled wheels dia.	1ft 11in.	1ft 10ins	2ft 9ins	2ft 9ins	2ft 8ins
Bogie wheel dia.	–	–	1fr 6½ins	1ft 4ins	1ft 4ins
Coupled wheelbase	4ft 2ins	4ft 4ins	5ft 6ins	5ft 10ins	5ft 6ins
Total wheelbase	4ft 2ins	4ft 4ins	13ft	12ft 4ins	16ft 6ins
Heating surface – tubes	108·5 sq ft	111 sq ft	168 sq ft	231sq ft	–
Heating surface – firebox	17·5 sq ft	20 sq ft	37 sq ft	23·5 sq ft	–
Heating surface – total	126 sq ft	131 sq ft	205 sq ft	254·3 sq ft	272 sq ft
Grate area	3·25 sq ft	3·5 sq ft	3·95 sq ft	5·6 sq ft	5·5 sq ft
Tank capacity	110 galls	110 galls	375 galls	396 galls	396 galls
Bunker capacity	3·5 cwt	3·5 cwt	15 cwt	15·7 cwt	15 cwt
Working pressure lbs per sq inch	150	160	160	178	175
Tractive force lbs	2970 @75%	–	5415 @75%	5510 @75%	–
Valve gear	Walschaerts	Walschaerts	Walschaerts	Walschaerts	Walschaerts
Brake	Hand	Hand	Steam & Hand	Steam & Hand	Steam & Hand
Firebox	Copper	Copper Belpaire	Copper Belpaire	Copper	Copper
Tubes	45 Steel	45 Brass	86 Brass	83 Brass	54 Brass
Tubes external dia. and length	1⅝ins x unknown	1⅝ins x 6ft	1½ins x unknown	1½ins x 7ft 2ins	2ins x 8ft 3ins
Width overall	5ft 8ins	5ft 5¼ins	6ft 3½ins	6ft 11ins	6ft 9ins
Height overall	8ft 8¾ins	8ft 4 11/16ins	8ft 11½ins	9ft 3¼ins	9ft 0ins
Length over buffers	15ft 5¼ins	14ft 2⅞ins	19ft 10¾ins	19ft 6⅛ins	–
Weight empty	5·75 tons	5·9 tons	10·9 tons	11·04 tons	–
Weight in working order	6·88 tons	7·0 tons	14·05 tons	14·7 tons	–
Max weight on a pair of wheels	2·38 tons	–	3·5 tons	3·46 tons	3·5 tons
Max weight per foot of wheelbase	1·65 tons	–	1·08 tons	1·14 tons	–
Max weight per foot run over buffers	0·446 tons	–	0·705 tons	–	–
Max weight on coupled wheels	6·88 tons	–	10·5 tons	10·35 tons	–

Note: The information in the table above is printed verbatim from the original. Some of the values given do not agree with those shown in other sources – so some care is advised in using what is shown.

CENTRES OF GRAVITY OF ROLLING STOCK		
LOCOS		
Baldwin	4-6-0	3ft 0ins in working order
Hunslet	4-6-0	2ft 10½ins in working order
American	2-6-2	2ft 10ins in working order
Barclay	0-6-0	2ft 9½ins in working order
Hudson	0-6-0	2ft 7½ins in working order
TRACTORS		
Simplex 20hp	0-4-0	1ft 4ins to 1ft 6ins
Simplex 40hp	0-4-0	1ft 4ins to 1ft 6ins
Petrol Electric	0-4-0	2ft 9ins
WAGONS		
Bogie well (with falling sides)		2ft 6¾ins
Bogie well (with stanchions)		2ft 9¾ins
Bogie open		2ft 11ins

The Hunslet 4-6-0T was a favourite of Light Railway Operating Companies but the manufacturer struggled to keep up with demand. See pages 146-155.

Note: the Baldwin diagram shows the cab side sheet cut-out as originally drawn and not as built. Given their reputation for instability, it is not surprising that the Baldwin locomotives come top of the above table. While the Hunslet design was only 1½ inches less, the position of the side tanks over the driving wheels made them more stable. See pages 156-163.

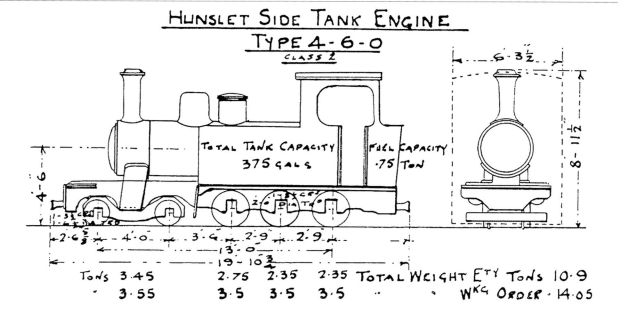

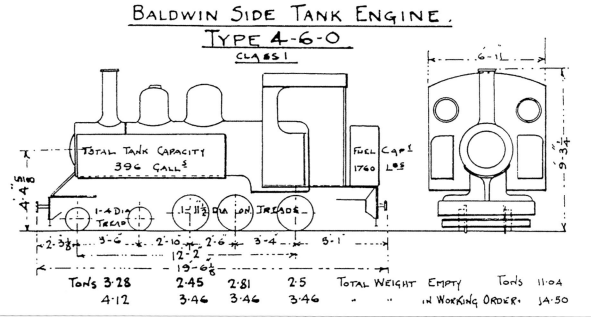

Collection: the late John Kimber & Australian Army History Unit

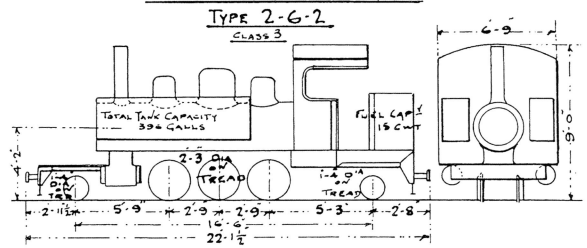

AMERICAN SIDE TANK ENGINE
TYPE 2·6·2
CLASS 3

TOTAL TANK CAPACITY 39° GALLS

FUEL CAP.Y 15 CWT

6·9

9·0

2·3 D/A ON TREAD

1·4·9 D/A ON TREAD

4·2

2·11½   5·9   2·9   2·9   5·3   2·8
16·6
22·1½

Left: The Alco 2-6-2T locomotives were the largest and most powerful on the WDLR. See pages 164-166.

Below left: The McEwan Pratt 10hp tractors were included, although, like the Hudson 0-4-0WT on page 226, it was very unlikely that Railway Operating troops would encounter either in the field. See page 168.

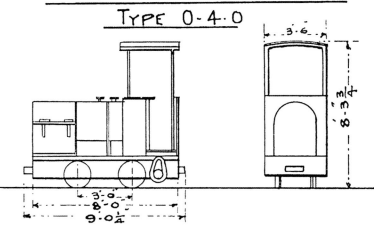

10 H P PETROL TRACTOR
TYPE 0·4·0

3·6

8·3¾

3·0
8·0
9·0¼

C Q LB   C Q LB
20.0.0 _ 17.3.0 TOTAL WEIGHT IN WORKING ORDER   T C Q 1 - 17 - 3

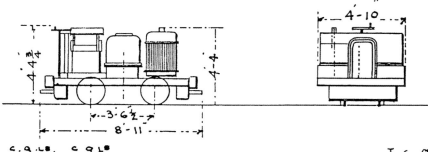

20 H P PETROL TRACTOR
TYPE 0·4·0.

4·10

4·4¾

4·4

3·6½
8·11

C Q LB   C Q LB
16.3.0   16.3.0 TOTAL WEIGHT EMPTY   T C Q 1 - 13 . 2
19.0.14   19.0.14 "   " IN WORKING ORDER WITH DRIVER 12ST. 1. 18. 1

Collection: the late John Kimber & Australian Army History Unit

40 H.P. PETROL TRACTOR.
TYPE 0-4-0.

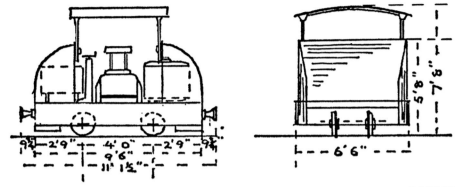

TONS 2.6625   2.8625 TOTAL WEIGHT EMPTY   5.725 TONS
  „   3.00   3.00   „   „ IN WORKING ORDER WITH DRIVER 12St. 6.00 „

CREWE (FORD) TRACTOR

* When on 13 arm wheels
   & loaded with Rail
   (60%) Equipment.

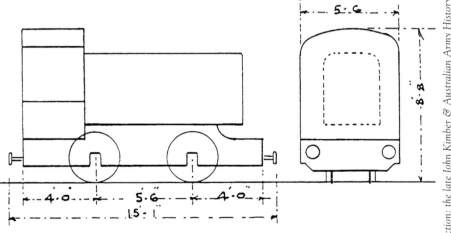

C. O. L.   C. O. L.   C. O. L.
9 . 21   9 . 3. 7   TOTAL WEIGHT 19 0. 0
7. 2. 7 & 14. 0. 0.   „   „   21. 2. 7 *

45 H.P. PETROL ELECTRIC TRACTOR
TYPE 0-4-0

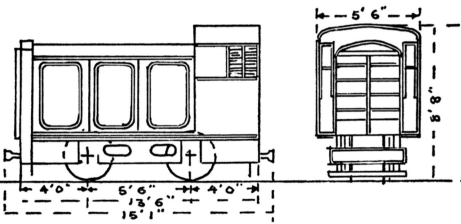

TONS 3¾   3¾   TOTAL WEIGHT EMPTY. 7.500 Tons
  „   4   4.   „.   (WORKING) 8.00 „.

PETROL ELECTRIC TRACTOR.
TYPE 0.4.0.

Collection: the late John Kimber & Australian Army History Unit

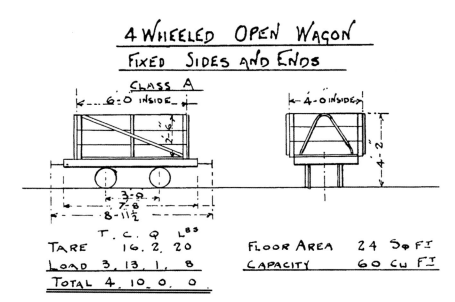

4 WHEELED OPEN WAGON
FIXED SIDES AND ENDS

CLASS A

	T. C. Q LBS
TARE	16. 2. 20
LOAD	3, 13, 1, 8
TOTAL	4. 10. 0. 0

FLOOR AREA 24 SQ FT
CAPACITY 60 CU FT

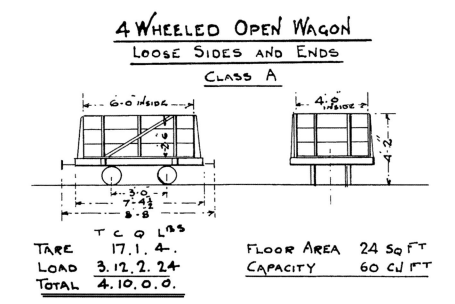

4 WHEELED OPEN WAGON
LOOSE SIDES AND ENDS
CLASS A

	T C Q LBS
TARE	17. 1. 4.
LOAD	3. 12. 2. 24
TOTAL	4. 10. 0. 0.

FLOOR AREA 24 SQ FT
CAPACITY 60 CU FT

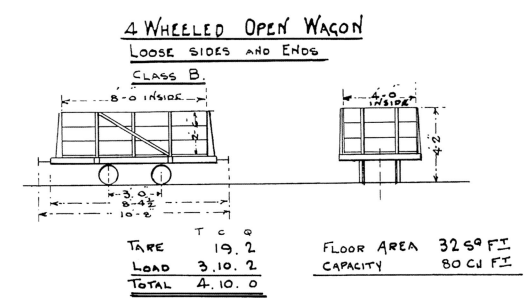

4 WHEELED OPEN WAGON
LOOSE SIDES AND ENDS
CLASS B.

	T C Q
TARE	19. 2
LOAD	3. 10. 2
TOTAL	4. 10. 0

FLOOR AREA 32 SQ FT
CAPACITY 80 CU FT

Above and right: The class 'A' wagons were the earliest supplied to the 60cm light railways in Flanders and went through a number of modifications. The enlarged class 'B' attempted to address these. See pages 182-184.

Page opposite left upper: The only diagram showing the 40HP Simplex tractors seem to be for the 'open' type – though overall dimensions are similar for all three types. Weights, however, particularly for the 'armoured' version, would be different to those shown in the diagram. Possibly there were diagrams for the 'protected' and 'armoured' type, but we did not find them in our searches. Note that both Simplex diagrams assume the weight in working order "with driver, 12 stone". See pages 168-173.

Page opposite upper right: The diminutive size of the Crewe Tractor compared to all the other WDLR locos and stock is readily apparent. See pages 178-181.

Page opposite lower: Two versions of the Petrol Electric Tractor diagram were found, the better detailed of them being for those built by British Westinghouse. Another diagram, for the Dick, Kerr does not carry so much information. Overall, the dimensions were the same for both types. See pages 174-177.

Collection: the late John Kimber & Australian Army History Unit

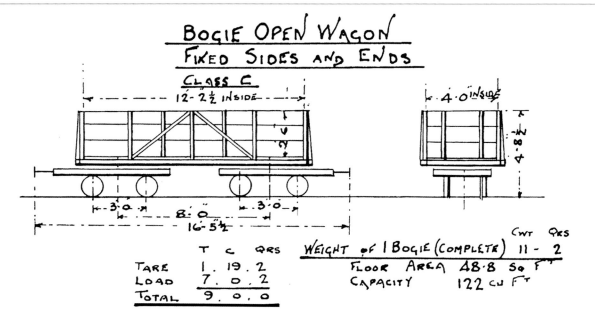

BOGIE OPEN WAGON
FIXED SIDES AND ENDS

CLASS C
12-2½ INSIDE
4·0 INSIDE
4·8

3·0   8·0   3·0
16-5½

TARE   1 . 19 . 2   T C QRS
LOAD   7 . 0 . 2
TOTAL   9 . 0 . 0

WEIGHT OF 1 BOGIE (COMPLETE) 11 - 2   CWT QRS
FLOOR AREA 48·8 SQ FT
CAPACITY   122 CU FT

The bogie class 'C' wagons incorporated parts from the 4w 'A' class. These included the chassis, which was adapted for use as a bogie. See pages 182-184.

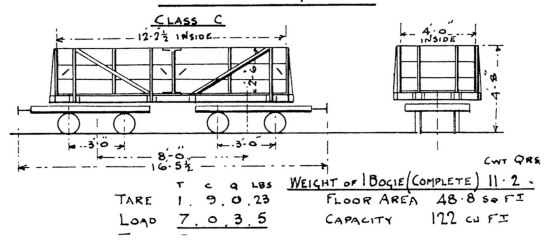

BOGIE OPEN WAGON
LOOSE SIDES AND ENDS

CLASS C
12-2½ INSIDE
4·0 INSIDE
2·6
4·8

3·0   8·0   3·0
16-5½

TARE   1 . 9 . 0 . 23   T C Q LBS
LOAD   7 . 0 . 3 . 5

WEIGHT OF 1 BOGIE (COMPLETE) 11·2   CWT QRS
FLOOR AREA 48·8 SQ FT
CAPACITY   122 CU FT

Collection: the late John Kimber & Australian Army History Unit

DETAILS OF 60cm WAGONS

	17ft Open Bogie Well wagon	17ft Open Bogie Wagon	12ft Open Bogie Wagon	12ft Open Bogie Wagon	8ft Open Bogie Wagon	6ft Open Bogie Wagon	6ft Bogie Open wagon	Well Wagon with detachable stanchions	Bogie Tank Wagon	Bogie Works Train Wagon
Capacity	225 cu.ft	175 cu.ft	122 cu.ft	122 cu.ft	80 cu.ft	60 cu.ft	60 cu.ft	–	1500 galls	–
Length inside	17ft 6ins	17ft 6ins	12ft 2½ins	12ft 2½ins	8ft 0ins	6ft 0ins	6ft 0ins	17ft 8½ins	17ft 8½ins	17ft 3ins
Width inside	4ft 9½ins	5ft 0ins	4ft 0ins	4ft 0ins	4ft 0ins	4ft 0ins	4ft 0ins	5ft 0ins	4ft 11⅝ins	4ft 11½ins
Depth inside	2ft 0ins	2ft 0ins	2ft 6ins	2ft 6ins	2ft 6ins	2ft 6ins	2ft 6ins	3ft 0ins	2ft 9ins	6ft 6ins
Length of well inside	7ft 4ins	–	–	–	–	–	–	7ft 4ins	–	–
Depth of well inside	1ft 7¾ins	–	–	–	–	–	–	1ft 7¾ins	–	–
Length over buffers	20ft 6½ins	20ft 6½ins	16ft 5½ins	16ft 5½ins	10ft 8ins	8ft 11½ins	8ft 8ins	20ft 6½ins	20ft 6½ins	20ft 6½ins
Width overall	5ft 4in	5ft 7in	4ft 8¼ins	4ft 8¼ins	4ft 8½ins	4ft 8½ins	4ft 8¼ins	5ft 5ins	5ft 6ins	5ft 4¾ins
Height from rail level	4ft 2⅞ins	4ft 2⅞ins	4ft 8¾ins	4ft 8½ins	4ft 2ins	4ft 2ins	4ft 2ins	5ft 2⅞ins	5ft 3⅞ins	9ft 1ins
Height from rail level to floor	2ft 2⅞ins	2ft 2⅞ins	2ft 2¾ins	2ft 2½ins	1ft 8in	1ft 8ins	1ft 8ins	2ft 2⅞ins	2ft 2⅞ins	2ft 5⅝ins
Height from rail to buffer centre	1ft 4ins	1ft 4ins	1ft 4ins	1ft 4ins	1ft 4ins	1ft 4ins	1ft 4ins	1ft 4ins	1ft 4ins	1ft 4ins
Wheelbase	3ft 0ins	3ft 0ins	3ft 0ins	3ft 0ins	3ft 0ins	3ft 0ins	3ft 0ins	3ft 0ins	3ft 0ins	3ft 0ins
Centres of bogies	13ft 9ins	13ft 9ins	8ft 0ins	8ft 0ins	–	–	–	13ft 9ins	13ft 9ins	13ft 9ins
Length of bogies	5ft 3ins	5ft 3ins	6ft 7ins	6ft 7ins	–	–	–	5ft 3ins	5ft 3ins	5ft 3ins
Width of bogies	3ft 2ins	3ft 2¼ins	3ft 6½ins	3ft 6½ins	–	–	–	3ft 2¾ins	3ft 2¾ins	3ft 2¾ins
Diameter of wheels	1ft 2ins	1ft 2ins	1ft 2ins	1ft 2ins	1ft 2ins	1ft 2ins	1ft 2ins	1ft 2ins	1ft 2ins	1ft 2ins
Diameter of wheel seat	2½ins	2½ins	2⅛ins	2⅛ins	2⅛ins	2⅛ins	2⅛ins	2½ins	2½ins	2½ins
Size of journals	4½ x 2ins	4½ x 2ins	4$\frac{5}{16}$ x 1¾ins	4$\frac{5}{16}$ x 1¾ins	4$\frac{5}{16}$ x 1¾ins	4$\frac{5}{16}$ x 1¾ins	4$\frac{5}{16}$ x 1¾ins	4½ x 2ins	4½ x 2ins	4½ x 2ins
Centres of bearing springs	–	–	2ft 9⅜ins	2ft 9⅜ins	2ft 9⅜ins	2ft 9⅜ins	2ft 9⅜ins	–	–	–
Tare: tons-cwts-qtrs-lbs	2-12-0-0	2-5-0-0	1-19-0-23	1-19-2-0	1-9-2-0	1-6-2-20	1-7-1-4	–	–	–
Load: tons-cwts-qtrs-lbs	9-8-0-0	9-8-0-0	7-0-3-5	7-0-2-0	3-10-2-0	3-3-1-3	3-12-2-4	–	–	–
Weight per axle on wheels	3-0-0-0	3-0-0-0	2-5-0-0	2-5-0-0	2-5-0-0	2-5-0-0	2-5-0-0	–	–	–
Gross weight per foot run over buffers	11-0-22	11-0-21	10-3-21	10-3-21	8-1-21	10-0-0	10-1-15	–	–	–
Proportion of load to tare	3·62 – 1	3·62 – 1	3·6 – 1	3·56 –1 / 3·62 – 1	4·4 – 1	4·21 – 1	–	–	–	–

Note: The information in the table above is printed verbatim from the original. Some of the values given do not agree with those shown in other sources, or even in the accompanying drawings – so care is advised in using what is shown. There were two other tables dealing with the loading of wagons. These are reproduced on page 192.

BOGIE LOW SIDED WAGON
WITH FALLING DOORS
CLASS D

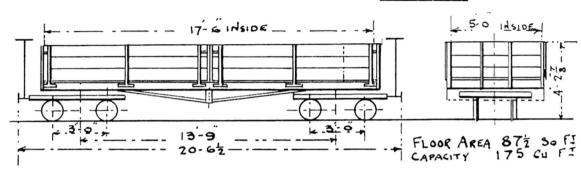

17'-6" INSIDE
5'-0 INSIDE
3'-0" 13'-9 3'-0"
20'-6½"
4'-2¾"

FLOOR AREA 87½ SQ FT
CAPACITY 175 CU FT

WOOD FRAME AND BOGIES			STEEL FRAME AND BOGIES		
	T	C	Q		T	C	Q
TARE	2. 7. 0.		TARE	2. 13. 0
LOAD	9. 13. 0.		LOAD	9. 7. 0
TOTAL	12. 0. 0		TOTAL	12. 0. 0

WEIGHT OF 1 WOOD BOGIE COMPLETE C. Q. LBS 11. 1. 24.
- " 1 STEEL - " 12. 0. 0

The bogie class 'D' was by far the most numerous of the WDLR wagons. The pair of drop-down side doors and removable centre post made the whole load area easily accessible. See pages 184-192.

The 'E' class was useful for bulk loads – such as fodder, though the central door made loading and unloading more difficult. See pages 184-196.

BOGIE OPEN WELL WAGON.
WITH CENTRE DOORS FALLING.
CLASS E.

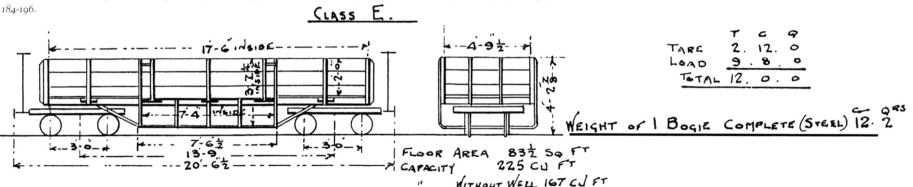

17'-6" INSIDE
4'-9½"
7'-4 WIDE
3'-0" 7'-6½" 3'-0"
13'-9
20'-6½"
4'-2¾"

	T	C	Q
TARE	2. 12. 0
LOAD	9. 8. 0
TOTAL	12. 0. 0

WEIGHT OF 1 BOGIE COMPLETE (STEEL) 12. 2 C. QRS

FLOOR AREA 83½ SQ FT
CAPACITY 225 CU FT
" WITHOUT WELL 167 CU FT

Collection: the late John Kimber & Australian Army History Unit

BOGIE WELL WAGON
WITH DETACHABLE STANCHIONS
CLASS F

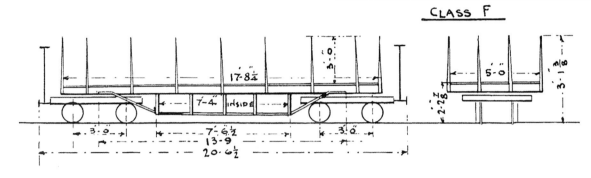

```
              T   C   Q
TARE      2.  8   1
LOAD      9. 11.  3
TOTAL    12   0   0
```

                                                    CWT QRS
WEIGHT OF 1 BOGIE COMPLETE (STEEL) 11-2

FLOOR AREA 88 SQ FT
CAPACITY (ASSUMED 323 CU FT)
WITHOUT USING WELL   265 CU FT

The bogie class 'F' was based on the 'E' but was essentially a flat wagon. See pages 196 and 92-98 for use as an artillery carrier.

The 'H' class tank wagon enabled clean water for drinking and the filling of steam locomotives to be delivered where needed. See pages 197-200.

TANK WAGON
CLASS H

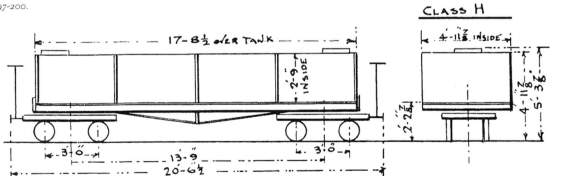

```
              TONS CWT QRS
TARE      3 - 18 - 3
LOAD      6 - 14 - 0
TOTAL    10 - 12 - 3.
```

                                                    CWT QRS
WEIGHT OF 1 BOGIE COMPLETE (STEEL) 12-1

CAPACITY   1500 GALLS

Collection: the late John Kimber & Australian Army History Unit

The Workshop Train was composed of six wagons in total, three with falling doors, two with double swing doors and one office wagon (see page opposite).

The whole train is described and illustrated on pages 201-213. There is a floor plan of the contents of each wagon on page 202.

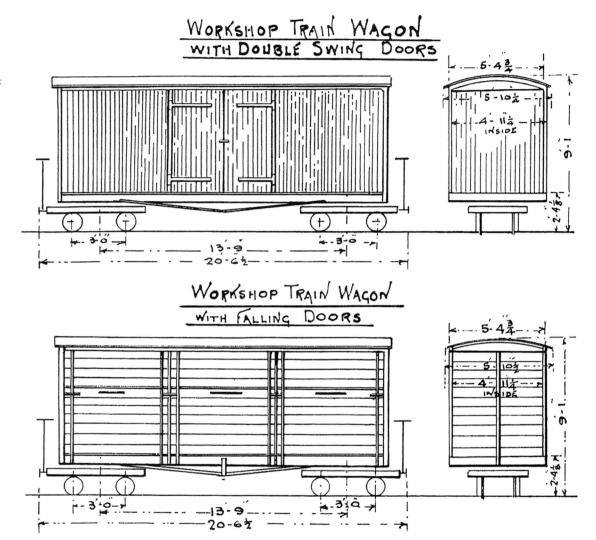

WORKSHOP TRAIN WAGON
WITH DOUBLE SWING DOORS

WORKSHOP TRAIN WAGON
WITH FALLING DOORS

Collection: the late John Kimber & Australian Army History Unit

WORKSHOP TRAIN OFFICE WAGON

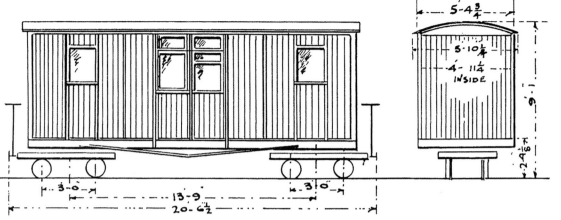

The Officer Wagon for the Workshop Train was the closest the WDLR ever got to a coach. See pages 205-213.

COVERED GOODS WAGON
WITH AMBULANCE FITTINGS

Although primarily described as a "Covered Goods Wagon", the size (particularly the width) would have made them awkward in general service. Most, if not all, were used as 'Ambulance Vans' see pages 214-216.

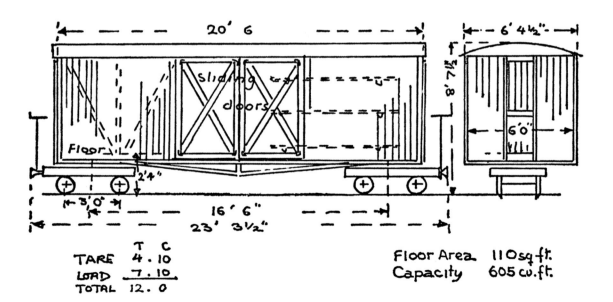

	T	C
TARE	4	10
LOAD	7	10
TOTAL	12	0

Floor Area 110 sq.ft.
Capacity 605 cu.ft.

Collection: the late John Kimber & Australian Army History Unit

CLASS L· WOODEN TIP·TRUCK

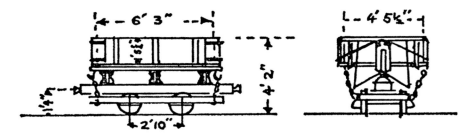

FLOOR AREA 28 sq ft   CAPACITY 40 cu ft.

DOUBLE SIDE TIP WAGON

CLASS K

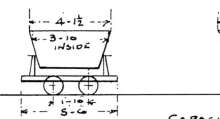

CAPACITY 18 CU FT

CLASS N.   HOPPER WAGON

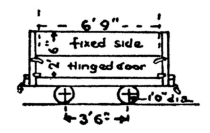

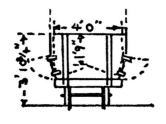

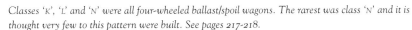

4 WHEELED LIGHT WAGON
WITH SLAT SIDES & ENDS
(FOR E·IN·C)
CLASS P

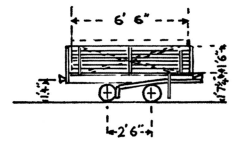

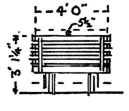

TARE   T. C. Q. L.
        - 8. 2. 0.

FLOOR AREA 26 sq ft.
CAPACITY of BOX. 39 cu ft
"
WITH PILED LOAD
of 5½" 50 cu ft.

Classes 'K', 'L' and 'N' were all four-wheeled ballast/spoil wagons. The rarest was class 'N' and it is thought very few to this pattern were built. See pages 217-218.

Class 'G' was a four-wheeled tank wagon – no diagram has been discovered for this type. See page 217.

There were no recorded class 'I', 'J' or 'O' type wagons – as these risked being mis-read as numerals.

Class 'P' came in a variety of forms from more than one manufacturer. See pages 219-222.

Collection: the late John Kimber & Australian Army History Unit

PROCESSING THE ALBUM PHOTOGRAPHS

A S MIGHT be expected after nearly a century of storage many of the photographs in the album are not in the best condition. Most pages have two 9 x 7 inch (whole plate) prints pasted in place and this has allowed a curl to develop which is hard to flatten for scanning. In addition, there are signs that the original processing was hurried.

Some prints are faded – like the image upper right – while a large number have patches of variable-sized white specks, marks and small hairs (or have been crudely re-touched), as below – see page 107.

Original scan – see page 155 for edited image. Many of the album photographs are dated and have brief descriptions. These are printed in bold type at the beginning of each caption – otherwise they are noted as 'untitled'.

None of this was judged satisfactory for reproduction, so a great deal of editing was required to achieve the results found on earlier pages. The primary scans were made using a Creo iQsmart flatbed repro scanner as 16bit RGB images, then processed in Adobe Photoshop CS6. Correcting faded prints (as above) was relatively easy, but cleaning up those that were badly marked often took over a day per image. Automatic removal of the blemishes would have degraded the clarity and sharpness of each image, so a great deal of hand work was required. This was undertaken using a Wacom digital tablet and pen. The computer platform throughout was an Apple Mac Pro G5.

Some of the original album pages contain two or more prints fixed together with fabric tape, to make a panorama. These were initially scanned as a group then each print scanned individually, for detail, so they might be reproduced separately. The cleaned-up images were saved in CMYK format for printing with a sepia tint.

THE GREAT WAR – A TRAIN OF EVENTS...

1914

June 28th — Francis Ferdinand assassinated at Sarajevo
July 5th — Kaiser William II promises German support for Austria against Serbia
July 28th — Austria declares war on Serbia
August 1st — Germany declares war on Russia
August 3rd — Germany declares war on France and invades Belgium (Schlieffen Plan)
August 4th — Britain declares war on Germany
August 23rd — The British Expeditionary Force retreats from Mons as Germany invades France
August 26th — Russian army defeated at Tannenburg and Masurian Lakes
September 6th — Battle of the Marne started
October 18th — First Battle of Ypres
October 29th — Turkey enters the war on Germany's side
Trench warfare begins on the Western Front

1915

January 19th — The first German Zeppelin raid on Britain
February 19th — Britain bombards Turkish forts in the Dardanelles
Spring — **Railway Operating Division (RE) formed, encompassing all British railway troops**
April 25th — Allied troops landed in Gallipoli
British Munitions Crisis
May 7th — The LUSITANIA sunk by a German U-boat
May 23rd — Italy declares war on Germany and Austria
August 5th — The Germans capture Warsaw
September 25th — Start of the Battle of Loos
December 19th — The Allies start the evacuation of Gallipoli

1916

January 27th — Conscription introduced in Britain
February 21st — Start of the Battle of Verdun

April — **Prototype Simplex Tractor sent to France for testing**
April 29th — British forces surrender to Turkish forces at Kut in Mesopotamia
March — **British use and expand former French 60cm lines**
War Office orders 60cm locos and stock
May 31st — Naval battle of Jutland
June 4th — Start of the Russian Brusilov Offensive
July 1st — Start of the Battle of the Somme
August — **British 'Programme A' contains more 60cm railway material**
August 10th — End of the Brusilov Offensive, Russian army in disarray
First Hunslet 4-6-0T locos sent to France
September 15th — First British use of tanks at the Somme
September 18th — **Sir Eric Geddes appointed Director General of Military Railways**
September 26th — **British 'Programme B' for extensive 60cm Light Railway equipment**
Autumn — **War Department Light Railways formed under Brigadier General Twining, RE**
December 7th — Lloyd George becomes British Prime Minister
December 12th — **British Central Light Railway Workshop sited at La Berguette**

1917

February 1st — Germany starts unrestricted submarine warfare campaign against Allied shipping
Baldwin 4-6-0T and Alco 2-6-2T start to arrive in quantity
April 6th — America declares war on Germany
April 16th — France launch an unsuccessful offensive

June — **Network of 60cm lines established in Flanders**
July 31st — Start of the Third Battle at Ypres
October 24th — Battle of Caporetto – the Italian Army heavily defeated
November 6th — Britain launches a major offensive on the Western Front
November 20th — British tanks win a victory at Cambrai
December 5th — Armistice between Germany and Russia signed
December 9th — British capture Jerusalem from the Turks

1918

March 3rd — The Treaty of Brest-Litovsk signed between Russia and Germany
March 21st — Germany break through on the Somme
March 29th — Marshall Foch appointed Allied Commander on the Western Front
April 9th — Germany start an offensive in Flanders
May 13th — **German advance forces evacuation of British Central Light Railway Workshop to Beaurainville**
July 15th — Second Battle of the Marne starts German army begins to collapse
August 8th — Allies begin successful counter attack and advance
September 19th — Turkish forces collapsed at Megiddo
September 29th — **British 60cm line to Passchendaele vital for ammunition supply due to poor conditions**
October 4th — Germany requests an armistice
October 29th — German Navy mutinies
October 30th — Turkey sues for peace
November 3rd — Austria sues for peace
November 9th — Kaiser William II abdicates
November 11th — Germany signs armistice with the Allies – the war ends

ACKNOWLEDGEMENTS

 NUMBER OF INDIVIDUALS AND ORGANISATIONS have been instrumental in the compilation of this book. Most deserving of mention is Colonel David W Ronald as, without him, this book would simply not exist. He rescued the main source and was generous enough to offer it for publication. His military experience and extensive knowledge on Army railway matters has been invaluable in compiling the text and captions.

Further valued assistance has been received from: Stuart Baker, Bob Barlow, Stuart Bennington (Australian War Memorial), Gerry Clark, Robert Gratton, Jim Hawkesworth, Jeremy Heil (Queen's University, Canada) Paul Ingham, Chris Jackson (Railway Gazette), the late John Kimber, Dr Roger Lee (Australian Army History Unit), Sam Maddra (Glasgow University Archives), Rita O'Donoghue (Imperial War Museum), David H Smith, Hazel Tomlinson (Hunslet Archive), John Townsend, Barry John Williams and Peter Wilson.

Images without credit are mainly from the album described on page xi or from the collection of Roy C Link.

BIBLIOGRAPHY

WDLR

The Railway Gazette, September 21, 1920, *Special War Transportation number*. O.O.P. – no ISBN.
Reprint: The Moseley Railway Trust, 2013 – ISBN 978-0-9540878-9-0

Transportation on the Western Front by A M Heniker (History of the Great War). 1st Edition 1937 O.O.P. – no ISBN.
Reprint: Imperial War Museum/The Battery Press – ISBN 0-89839-172-2

Light Railways of the First World War by W J K Davies. David & Charles, Newton Abbot 1967 O.O.P. – no ISBN.

Railway and War Before 1918 by D Bishop & W J K Davies. Blandford Press 1972 O.O.P. – ISBN 0-7137070-3-8

Narrow Gauge at War by Keith Taylorson. Plateway Press 1987. – ISBN 1-871980-57-7

Narrow Gauge at War 2 by Keith Taylorson. Plateway Press 1996 – ISBN 1-871980-29

The Light Track from Arras by T R Heritage. Plateway Press 1999 O.O.P. – ISBN 1-871980-40-2

Hunslet 1215 by I G Hughes. The Oakwood Press 2010 – ISBN 978-0-85361-709-9

GENERAL HISTORY

Manual of Field Works – *all Arms,* 1st edition, Her Majesty's Stationary Office, 1921 (provisional), O.O.P. – no ISBN.
Reprint: The Naval & Military Press Ltd – no ISBN.

The First World War – *an illustrated history* by Hew Strachan. Simon & Shuster 2003 – ISBN 0-7432-3959-8

World War One – *a chronological narrative* by Phillip Warner. Pen & Sword Books 2008 – ISBN 978-1-84415-776-1

The Western Front Companion – *the complete guide to how the armies fought for four devastating years, 1914-1918* by Mark Adkin. Aurum Press 2013 – ISBN 978-1-84513-710-6

NOTES

1 inch	25.43 millimetres
12 inches = 1 foot	0.304 metres
3 feet = 1 yard	0.194 metres
22 yards = 1 chain	20.11 metres
1760 yards = 1 mile	1.60 kilometres
1 cubic yard	0.765 cubic metres
1 acre	0.40 hectares
1 gallon	4.536 litres
1 ton	1.01 tonnes
¼d = 1 farthing (d)	0.104 pence (p)
1 old penny (d)	0.416 pence (p)
12 pennies = 1 shilling (s)	5 pence (p)
2 shillings (s)	10 pence (p)
5 shillings (s)	25 pence (p)
10 shillings (s)	50 pence (p)
240 pennies = 1 pound (£)	1 pound (£)
21 shillings = 1 guinea	1 pound, 5 pence

To appreciate financial details in the text the multiplier given below allows the costs at the time to be compared with present day values.

Year	Multiplier
1886-1901	45
1902-1914	40
1915	30
1916-1917	25
1918-1919	20
1920-1921	15
1922-1926	20
1927-1939	25

INDEX

"**Yesterday** I visited the battlefield of last year. The place was scarcely recognisable. Instead of a wilderness of ground torn up by shell, the ground was a garden of wild flowers and tall grasses. Most remarkable of all was the appearance of many thousands of white butterflies which fluttered around. It was as if the souls of the dead soldiers had come to haunt the spot where so many fell. It was eerie to see them. And the silence! It was so still that I could almost hear the beat of the butterflies' wings."

Unnamed British officer in 1919.